Self-Emptying Love in a Global Context

The Spiritual Exercises and the Environment

Robert T. Sears, SJ, and
Joseph A. Bracken, SJ

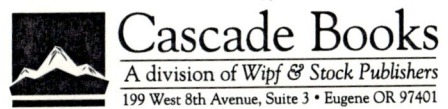

SELF-EMPTYING LOVE IN A GLOBAL CONTEXT
The Spiritual Exercises and the Environment

Copyright © 2006 Robert T. Sears, SJ, and Joseph A. Bracken, SJ. All rights reserved. Except for brief quotations in critical publications or reviews, no part of this book may be reproduced in any manner without prior written permission from the publisher. Write: Permissions, Wipf & Stock, 199 W. 8th Ave., Eugene, OR 97401.

ISBN: 1-59752-559-6

Cataloging-in-Publication data

Sears, Robert T. (Robert Thomas), 1934–
Self-emptying love in a global context : the spiritual exercises and the environment / Robert T. Sears, SJ, and Joseph A. Bracken, SJ.

vi + 88 p. 20 cm.

ISBN 1-59752-559-6 (alk. paper)
1. Spiritual Exercises. 2. Environmentalism. 3. Ignatius, of Loyola, Saint, 1491–1556. 4. Jesuits—Spiritual Life. I. Title. II. Bracken, Joseph A.

BX3703 B74 2006

Manufactured in the U.S.A.

Contents

Introduction / v

1 The Environment in Theological History / 1

The Origin of the Two Themes in Scripture / 1

The Ambiguity in the Early Writers / 9

Augustine: A Bridge between These Two Positions / 12

Medieval Scholasticism / 16

Thomas Aquinas: The Goal of Human Redemption / 18

Francis of Assisi: All Creation as God's Family / 20

Summary and Focus: A Resurrection Approach to the Environment / 22

2 ENVIRONMENT IN THE SPIRITUAL EXERCISES / 27

Principle and Foundation / 28

Meditations of the First Week / 34

Call of the King and the Environment / 40

The King's Way as Our Way:
Incarnation and Nativity / 47

Christ's Public Life and
the Ignatian Strategy / 52

The Election / 58

The Passion: In Labor with God / 60

The Resurrection / 64

Contemplation to Attain God's Love / 72

Conclusion / 80

Bibliography / 85

Introduction

DAVID Toolan has reflected on the changing cosmology of modern science and our need to care for our increasingly devastated earth.[1] As he succinctly put it: "you cannot defend defenseless embryos, have a 'consistent ethic of life,' or make a 'preferential option for the poor' without simultaneously deciding to do justice to the ravaged and defenseless 'commons' of the globe: Earth, water, and air."[2] This should seem obvious in today's context; but for several reasons, it seems still not to be really operative in our thinking and action. Part of the reason for our inattention to nature is theological.

In a much debated article on the cause of our modern day assault on nature, Lynn White blamed Christianity in large part for the pernicious anthropocentric attitudes behind it.[3] Drew Christiansen pointed out that most theologians went along with White's analysis, whereas nonbelievers argued that

---

[1] David Toolan, SJ, "'Nature Is a Heraclitean Fire': Reflections on Cosmology in an Ecological Age," *Studies in the Spirituality of the Jesuits* 23/5 (November 1991).
[2] Ibid., 6.
[3] Lynn White, "Historical Roots of Our Ecological Crisis," *Science* 155 (1967) 1203–7.

the final culprit was impersonal science, which, in the wake of Descartes' and Newton's "objective world" had felt no qualms about exploiting nature.[4] Still, Christianity was not without influence in that it has tended to focus so much on human salvation that nature was relegated to a very secondary position.

This was the view prominent in the time of Ignatius. He was touched by contemplation of the stars, and strove to "find God's Love in all things." Yet how many of us think of care for the Earth in light of the *Spiritual Exercises*? Do we not rather see the Earth (as one of God's creatures along with "the other things on the face of the earth") as something to be indifferent to and to use only insofar as it helps us toward our salvation? How can we bring awareness of the environment into our Ignatian spirituality and gain a passion for its healing and wholeness as integral to the redemption of people? That is the challenge this essay addresses.

We begin this study by considering the ambiguous legacy of our Judeo-Christian theology in relation to the environment prior to St. Ignatius. What views influenced him and what changes are called for today? In chapter 2 we examine the *Spiritual Exercises* more closely in light of this analysis to see how they might be understood to include care for the environment.

---

[4] See Drew Christiansen, "Notes on Moral Theology," *Theological Studies* 51 (1990) 64–81.

Chapter One

The Environment in Theological History

IN a book investigating Christianity's attitude toward nature, H. Paul Santmire analyzed two main theological themes: the one seeing spirituality as an ascent to God transcending nature and this life, the other seeing the very fruitfulness of nature as a sign of God's presence and offering the goal of human endeavor as the "promised Land."[1] He argues persuasively that it is the first view that was predominant in Christian theology up to modern times, and it leaves very little room for care of the Earth.

The Origin of the Two Themes in Scripture

Ascent Spirituality

The ascent spirituality has roots in a certain interpretation of the Old Testament that sees it

---

[1] See H. Paul Santmire, *The Travail of Nature: The Ambiguous Ecological Promise of Christian Theology* (Philadelphia: Fortress, 1985). This is his more detailed study from which we will cite in this essay. He has updated his approach more recently in *Nature Reborn: The Ecological and Cosmic Promise of Christian Theology* (Minneapolis: Fortress, 2000).

basically as centered on God's covenant with humans with the rest of creation as a kind of backdrop.[2] The Israelites' notion of creation follows on their experience of redemption. Israel first experienced God forming them as a people and governing their history, but it gradually became clear to them that the very God who governs them is creator of the whole universe. Creation is servant of redemption. God's revelation to Israel came primarily not through the natural order, as with the surrounding countries, but through the divine election and deliverance from Egypt and through the Sinai covenant. In fact, Israel viewed nature cults as an enemy. Only by acknowledging God as Lord of history could Israel then view the natural order as pointing to its maker and therefore "good." Lampe admits that the *eschaton* "involves all of God's world, but it does so because a transformed world is included in the realization of God's creative and redemptive purpose for his people."[3]

The New Testament continues this anthropocentric focus, only now Christ is the center. There is also a similar progression: first the experience of the Lordship of Christ, then his Lordship over all kingdoms, and finally over the whole creation from beginning to end. In fact, Lampe holds (with Karl Barth) that *ktisis* (creation) in the New Testament refers primarily to

---

[2] See G. W. H. Lampe, "The New Testament Doctrine of *ktisis*," *Scottish Journal of Theology* 17 (1964) 449–62.
[3] Ibid., 453.

humankind, and only secondarily is it extended to animals and inanimate nature created for humanity's sake. Even Paul's reference to "creation groaning" is incidental to his praises of God's work in human redemption. The renewal of sinful humankind is primary, even in Colossians 1:15-20 ("firstborn of all creation"); the author looks back to original creation only to see Christ as its historical fulfillment.[4]

This ascent view of creation is shared by many other Protestant exegetes besides Lampe (G. Ernest Wright, Rudolf Bultmann, Gerhard von Rad, etc.) and is evidenced in Aquinas, Bonaventure, and even Teilhard de Chardin. It has become a dominant spiritual perspective throughout the history of Christian theology. God has descended in Christ in order to divinize us that we might ascend to God. How creation relates to this fulfillment is not attended to—certainly not creation as we now experience it.

Ecological Spirituality

Yet an ascent view of creation is not the only possible perspective in scripture. Santmire sees two other experiences (metaphors)—that of the fecundity of nature and the journey to the promised land—that coalesce in an "ecological motif" where a renewed Earth is equally central in the *eschaton*. This view need not be opposed to the

---
[4] Ibid., 459.

anthropocentric perspective in Scripture, but broadens it to include nature.

Walter Brueggemann countered the human-centered imbalance with his study *The Land: Place as Gift, Promise, and Challenge in Biblical Faith*.[5] He points out how especially in Deuteronomy, the land is regarded as a gift from God. It does not belong to Israel. It is not merely a means for human use. "The land is mine and you are but aliens who have become my tenants" (Leviticus 25:23). This is an abundant, fruitful land "flowing with milk and honey" (Deuteronomy 26:9, etc.). If the Israelites serve Yahweh faithfully, abundant blessings will be poured out on the land and animals (Deuteronomy 28). The Lord will open up the heavens to provide rain, and thus blessed, the Israelites will lend to the nations and not borrow. But, if they do not obey the divine precepts, the Lord will send curses, confusion, and frustration (Deuteronomy 28:20-21) and the land will be taken away. The two themes of land and fruitfulness are thus joined with the theme of election in Deuteronomy. We see a celebration of God's rule not just over humans, but over the land. "The earth is Yahweh's and the fullness thereof" (Psalm 24:1). This focus on the land is highlighted in the Yahwist and Priestly creation accounts. It is Yahweh who has Adam name the creatures

---

[5] See Walter Brueggemann, *The Land: Place as Gift, Promise, and Challenge in Biblical Faith,* Overtures to Biblical Theology (Minneapolis: Fortress, 2002 [1st ed. 1977]), esp. chapter 4: "Reflection at the Boundary."

(Genesis 2–3) and who gives dominion over the creatures to the man and woman (Genesis 1). Thus, we find Israel's awareness of Yahweh's rule over the land in monarchical and postmonarchical periods.

The question exegetes are faced with is whether these elements of creation are imported from surrounding cultures, or whether they spring from Israel's founding experience of Yahweh's call. What seems clear is that even if Israel had no creation account apart from God's election in this early period, it also had no redemption without creation. What we find is Yahweh as "Lord of heaven and earth." The very name Yahweh seems to be derived from a cultic epithet referring to *El* as "the one who brings into existence all that exists."[6] Yahweh's actions bringing Israel out of Egypt by parting the sea show Yahweh's power over creation. Thus Psalm 29, which celebrates Yahweh's power in thunderstorm and mountains, is not borrowed from Canaan, but is linked to the Sinai tradition. One cannot separate Israel's foundational election faith from faith in the Creator. It is primarily faith in Yahweh as gracious Lord of power that freed Israel. This is in continuity with the later flowering of creation faith in Isaiah and the Priestly tradition.

Focus on Yahweh as *universal* Creator appears especially during the Exile. In their time of

---

[6] See George Landes, "Creation and Liberation," *Union Seminary Quarterly Review* 33 (1978) 80.

deepest despair, the prophets announced God's judgment on Israel but also God's promise of renewed land and indeed a universally renewed earth. Second Isaiah (Isaiah 40–55) proclaims that Yahweh is doing "a new thing" (Isaiah 43:19): making rivers in the desert, creating jackals and ostriches who honor Yahweh, that my chosen people "might declare my praise." Third Isaiah (Isaiah 56–66) expands this hope to the whole earth, totally beyond this world (Isaiah 65:17-25, etc.). Thus, Yahweh's power over the beginning of the earth reaches out to a future restoration of all creation.

The New Testament witness can also be read in this ecological light, even though the renewal of creation is never separated from the conversion and renewal of humankind. Despite the difficulties of getting at the actual "historical Jesus," each Gospel writer makes it clear that Jesus was seen as the promised Messiah, who would bring to fulfillment the apocalyptic expectations of Israel. The Kingdom of God was made present in his ministry (see Mark 1:14: "Repent and believe, the kingdom of God is at hand," etc.). His giving sight to the blind and hearing to the deaf and other healings revealed this eschatological Kingdom, as did his reconciling the poor (Isaiah 29:18-19). His power over nature, his forming a new community of twelve, his feeding the multitudes and establishing the Eucharist revealed the promised Kingdom (Isaiah 25:6-8). The God Jesus called "Abba" with such intimacy, was not just the God of individuals or even of the whole people of Israel. He was the maker of heaven and earth (e.g., Our Father "on earth as in heaven," "the sun shining on good and bad," "no sparrow falls without Abba's leave," etc.). Jesus' God, who is the ultimate judge of living and dead, and the one who will finally come to judge the world (Matthew 24:34-35), is also ruler of heaven and earth.

This apocalyptic vision of cosmic renewal can be seen in Paul (see Romans 8:19-20: "all creation waits with eager longing for the revealing of the children of God"; also 1 Corinthians 15: 20-28, etc.). It is the view of Colossians (1:15-20, etc.) and Ephesians (1:20-23, etc.), and of the book of Revelation where the heavenly Jerusalem descends to earth in the midst of a renewed creation (Revelation 21:1-4). Jesus' resurrection Lordship is coextensive with God's, for through him all things were created (John 1:1, etc.) and in him all will come to final judgment.

In the time between the beginning and the final consummation, the disciples are sent to preach the Good News to the ends of the earth (Matthew 28:18-20; Acts 1:1-8). Thus, as Santmire says: "No biblically legitimate creation theology or cosmic Christology will prompt its adherents to forsake the life and mission of the people of God under the cross."[7] It is this essential focus on the need for human conversion in

---

[7] See Santmire, *Travail of Nature*, 209.

light of the cross that seems to have given rise in the tradition to seeing human salvation as primary, to the neglect of the restoration of creation. Santmire sees the beginning of this separation in the Gospel of John and the Epistle to the Hebrews. For even though John sees Jesus' role in creation, he has a descending and ascending view akin to the spiritualizing tendency in later theology. Thus, Jesus "comes from above" (John 3:31), and his followers "are not of this world" (John 17:14). Jesus prays not for the world, but for these chosen followers; so the focus seems to be a renewed community with little attention to a renewed creation.

Similarly in Hebrews, Christ is a high priest in a heavenly sanctuary (8:1-2) who came to earth to abolish the old sacrificial rites and returned as he "passed through the heavens" (4:14). The figure of Christ thus exemplifies a "descending-ascending" spirituality influenced by Greek thinking, [8] The Old Testament saints were "strangers and pilgrims on the earth" (11:13) who looked forward to a city "whose builder and maker is God" (11:10,16; 13:14). The author uses the image of a pilgrimage to a good land, but attaches a purely spiritual meaning to it. The goal is the "heavenly Jerusalem" (12:22-23), but without solidarity with the whole creation as we find in

---

[8] See Edward Schillebeeckx, *Jesus: An Experiment in Christology*, trans. Hubert Hoskins (New York: Crossroads, 1981) 275.

Paul. This city does not descend to earth, but Christians are to *ascend* to it.

Thus, Scripture itself leaves the fate of creation in a certain ambiguity. Is creation to be transformed with humans, or are humans transformed through creation but ultimately apart from it? Much of the following tradition chose the second option as we will see. Which perspective was operative in Ignatius (or could be operative in light of today's view) remains to be seen.

The Ambiguity in the Early Writers

Irenaeus (c. 130–200) and Origen (c. 185–254) are early examples of different approaches to the role of creation in salvation history. Irenaeus opposed the Gnostics for many reasons, but especially for their rejection of the Creator God of the Old Testament and for their postulate of a passive God utterly removed from the material order. He saw nature in light of Scripture as humanity's God-given home—blessed, embraced, and cared for by God. His theology is a kind of "creation history," in which the Logos becomes flesh and moves creation to its God-intended fulfillment. This fulfillment, Irenaeus seems to presuppose, would have eventuated whether or not Adam had sinned, and Jesus would have been its culmination. Creation has not fallen, according to Irenaeus, but it does need perfecting. So the incarnate Word or Logos of the Creator, Christ, recapitulates what has gone before in the history of creation. He thereby both overcomes the distortions of sin which entered through Adam, and also carries the whole history of creation one final step further toward the final consummation through his resurrection. In the final consummation "Neither the substance nor the essence of the creation will be annihilated . . . but 'the fashion' of the world passes away."[9]

For Irenaeus the work of creation is focused on humans. "Humans were not made for creation but creation for humans."[10] Yet the "sole purpose" of creation is not just to set a stage for humans. All is one, and all is fulfilled together. His final Kingdom vision is the human set in the center of a renewed creation, blessed with abundance "when also the creation, having been renovated and set free, shall fructify with an abundance of all kinds of food, from the dew of heaven, and from the fertility of the earth."[11] This new creation will be permanent, "as Isaiah declares."[12] Thus, in Irenaeus' view, the full revelation of God is the whole renewed creation in which humans will praise the glory of God in the abundant richness and fertility of creation. He represents the "ecological theme" very fully, while not negating the centrality of humans in creation.

---

[9] Irenaeus, *Against the Heresies* 5.23.2.
[10] Irenaeus 5.29.1 "non enim homo propter illam [creation], sed conditio facta est propter hominem"; trans. by Santmire, *Travail of Nature*, 41.
[11] Irenaeus 5.33.3.
[12] Irenaeus 5.36.1.

The Environment in Theological History

For Origen, on the contrary, the situation is quite different. His theology was influenced by the hierarchical world view of neo-Platonism and Plotinus. Initially the unchanging One, God, dwelled above in eternity, surrounded by a world of rational spirits (*logikoi*), whom God created eternally to live in perfect communion with God. As free spirits, some turned from God and fell toward nonbeing. God created the material-vital world as a gracious act to "stop" their fall by encasing them, as it were, in matter. God creates the world as an ordered hierarchy of being, and the fallen spiritual beings take their places in gradated positions from the highest heavens (sun, moon, and stars above) to the human level. Origen understands Romans 8 as saying all rational spirits "groan for their own liberation."[13] Thus, material creation is a gracious act of God, but ultimately it results from the fall. Evil does not reside in matter, yet matter is "only for the purpose of educating humanity, through trials and tribulations, to return to a higher incorporeal, spiritual destiny."[14]

As a consequence, the ultimate goal of divine providence in Origen will be the return of all rational creatures to their original state in eternity. The material world will seemingly "fall back into

---

[13] Origen, *Commentary on Romans IV*; quoted by Thomas E. Clarke, *The Eschatological Transformation of the Material World according to St. Augustine* (Woodstock, Md.: Woodstock College Press, 1956) 7.

[14] See Santmire, *Travail of Nature*, 50.

nothingness, from whence it came."[15] Our resurrection bodies will be so refined physically that they will have lost their corporality. Thus Origen is a clear example of "ascent spirituality." He speaks of the ascent of the soul from the Egypt of this world to the Promised Land above, "to the fatherland in paradise," but this is clearly a symbolic land, freed of materiality. In Origen the exalted Good triumphs over the fertile Goodness of God. Human life in nature is something to be overcome and left behind in order to unite with the immutable, immaterial One.

Augustine: A Bridge between These Two Positions

Augustine (354–430) was brought up by his Christian mother, but joined the disciples of Mani in his early youth. Manichaean dualism and the view of the material world as evil, then, shaped his thinking. Gradually, however, he fell under the influence of Plotinus with his view of God's overflowing goodness and more positive view of the world. His thought developed further through the influence of Scripture and of the Donatist Tyconius, an African theologian wholly influenced by biblical ideas, who owed nothing to classical culture or philosophy. It was this biblical influence, according to Santmire, that moved Augustine increasingly in the direction of Irenaeus, with special attention to history and

---

[15] Ibid., 51.

eschatology in his later years. Unlike Origen, he then saw the final goal of creation as blessed by the overflowing goodness of God, a "new heaven and a new earth," that is not a return to the beginning, but an expression of God's superabundant goodness.[16]

Augustine speaks of God's action in creation as both creator and sustainer. As creator all things are created good (including human nature and will). There is no manichaean dualism in the mature Augustine. Every creature, from the least to the greatest, is needed for the beauty and harmony of the whole creation. Augustine chides the "heretics" who question the utility of fire, frost, wild beasts, frogs, etc. "They do not consider how admirable these things are in their own places, how excellent in their own natures, how beau-

---

[16] Ibid., 59. Drew Christiansen questions Augustine's ecological focus in his contribution to "Notes on Moral Theology," *Theological Studies* 51 (1990) 72–74. He agrees that Augustine gained a respect for the diversity of God's creatures as well as humans. Yet does contemplation of the goodness of creation displace the orientation to God as the Good or the goal of human life? Augustine's delight in the natural world wanes with his passing years, according to Peter Brown, and he writes much more of angels than of plants and animals and landscapes. And Augustine's view of life in the world remained a *peregrinatio* or that of a resident alien who longed for the heavenly Jerusalem. Christiansen questions whether such a view would provide a basis for modern day environmental ethics. Finally, Augustine's later view does move in the direction of God as "overflowing goodness"; yet even though life with God is a social life with the saints, it is still union with God. The goodness of creation is meant to draw humanity to God—this is no wholesale rejection of "ascent."

tifully adjusted to the rest of creation, and how much grace they contribute to the universe by their own contributions . . . ."[17] All things are said by Genesis to be "very good." Augustine never deviates from this, even refusing to speak of the earth as fallen with humans or as being under the power of evil. Satan has no hold over the physical world or any part of it, but only over sinful, unbelieving humanity.[18]

Further, God sustains all things by being forever present and active. God is omnipotent, not by arbitrary power (*potentia temeraria*) but by the power of wisdom (*sapientiae virtute*). God governs all things "in such a way that he allows them to function and behave in ways proper to them."[19] God broods over the world with the warmth of the Holy Spirit, ruling and containing all things effortlessly, without labor, bringing the "seeds" of creation to life each at the proper time. In the end, the whole history of creation will come to rest, "totally renewed in eternity with God, following a universal conflagration of all things."[20] Augustine joins Irenaeus in this view, integrating the ideas of cosmic renewal and the resurrection of the body.[21] And despite Augustine's psychological alienation from the body and sexuality, his developed thought moves in a different direction.

---

[17] See *City of God*, 12.22.
[18] See Clarke, *The Eschatological Transformation*, 35.
[19] *City of God*, 7.30.
[20] Santmire, *Travail of Nature*, 64.
[21] See *City of God*, 20.16.

The body is good, a home, friend, spouse, and will be fully resurrected and glorified, including its sex organs. It is not the body that is evil, but the will.[22]

Augustine still maintains a certain hierarchy in nature, but seems to downplay the "dominion" text in Genesis. He interprets that text as human reason and intelligence excelling all the creatures of earth, air, and sea. His focus is on God's rule, and God's rule, as we said, is gracious and empowers creatures to be according to their own natures. Domination, or ruling over, is a mark of *fallen* human nature. Now animals live more peaceably with their own kind than with humans, who were supposed to encourage concord.[23] The rightful relationship of humanity with nature is solidarity and peace rather than disjunction and domination.[24]

Thus, for Augustine, creation springs from the overflowing goodness of God (adapting Plotinus) initiating, accompanying and bringing it to a final glorious fulfillment in union with the resurrected Christ. For Origen, material creation was a kind of stage to catch fallen rational spirits. For Augustine it is part of God's original creation, and will be included in the final glorification which God is presently bringing about through the work of grace.

---

[22] See *City of God*, 14.3.
[23] Ibid., 12.22.
[24] Ibid., 19.12-13.

Medieval Scholasticism

As Christian history unfolded, Augustine's position became the dominant force in the West; yet his later view of the resurrection of nature as well as of human beings was not included. Santmire presents several reasons for this. An important factor was the influence of Dionysius the Areopagite (ca. 500) as translated by John Scotus Erigena (ca. 810–877). Erigena saw theology as a branch of wisdom which speculated about the divine nature. True philosophy was true religion for him, and he was influenced by the hierarchical system of Dionysius and Origen. Like Origen, he taught that God had not originally intended his creative power to extend down as far as corruptible matter. Humans originally were to be without bodily needs, and even sexual differentiation was a "punishment of sin."[25] Only after the fall was matter created to contain the fall, and in the end it will be abolished and humans resurrected in a wholly spiritual, sexless state. Erigena was condemned in his day as rationalizing the faith, but the perspective and questions he raised remained for later theology.

Another influence on Medieval theology was the monastic tradition of Benedict (ca. 480–550). He added to the earlier contemplative, liturgical approach a communal structure and focus on

---

[25] See Jaroslav Pelikan, *The Christian Tradition: A History of the Development of Doctrine* (Chicago: University of Chicago Press, 1971–89) 3:95–105, on John Scotus Erigena. Also, Santmire, *Travail of Nature*, 77–78.

work. Ora et Labora (pray and work) was his vision, as Santmire says: "prompted by an evangelical sense of mission, communities of Benedictines did go out into the wilderness areas of Europe and work to tame nature, sometimes with dramatic results, for the purpose of their own survival and as a praise-offering to God."[26] Irish monasticism, and their missionaries, also carried the ideal of the saint taming the wilderness and befriending the animals like Adam and Eve in paradise—another sort of reclaiming nature. This sense of cooperative mastery over nature was neither passive contemplation nor thoughtless exploitation, but it heralded a change in perspective in which we can see the seeds of modern science.

Thirdly, with the rise of Mariology and the cult of courtly love, there was also a rebirth of attention to nature and the "Goddess Natura." Key to this resurgence was the power of the concept of the "hierarchy of being," not unlike the dynamism of the concept of evolution in the time of Darwin. Together with this structured view of nature was the popularity of the view of the human creature as a "microcosm" (also from Erigena). Now humans were not only in the image of God, but also in the image of the cosmos—a kind of world in miniature. That made study of nature a kind of study of oneself—both reflecting the beautiful order created by God. At the same time, however, it was more a contemplative than

---

[26] See Santmire, *Travail of Nature*, 78.

an historical order—modeled more on Platonic ideas than on Irenaeus' and Augustine's view of salvation history.

Thomas Aquinas: The Goal of Human Redemption

Thomas Aquinas (1225–1274) brought some conceptual clarity to these various tendencies, but also continued and even solidified the ambiguity regarding nature. On the one hand he had a "radical optimism" about nature's goodness in itself.[27] On the other hand, in the final consummation animals, plants and minerals will not be included since they are no longer needed for resurrected human life and sub-human creation is created for the purpose of serving human life.[28]

In creation, Thomas focuses on God's transcendent freedom and efficient causality, though some traces of emanation-participation remain in the notion of analogy. In governance, God is present in all things, keeping them in existence; but God "governs some things by means of others," according to their place in the hierarchy of being.[29] This is a sign of God's dignity, according to Thomas, but it clearly qualifies God's immanence and makes it difficult for Thomas to convey

---

[27] See Etienne Gilson, *The Christian Philosophy of St. Thomas Aquinas*, trans. L. K. Shook (New York: Random House, 1956) 189.
[28] See Thomas Aquinas, *Summa Theologica*, 3 Supp 91.5; quoted in Santmire, *Travail of Nature*, 94
[29] See *Summa Theologica* 1.103.6.

the powerful immediacy and gentle care of the Creator for creation as Augustine and Irenaeus did. Although the variety and multiplicity of nature is needed to express the infinite goodness of God,[30] all subhuman creatures exist for the sake of higher creatures—"lifeless beings exist for living beings, plants for animals, and the latter for man." This means "that the whole of material nature exists for man, inasmuch as he is a rational animal."[31] In other words, God's focus is on saving humans, and all else is subordinated to that.

This becomes clear when Thomas speaks of the final end of all things. Thomas sees humanity alone as created in a "state of grace." The universe pertains to the "first perfection" of creation, when God rested on the seventh day, whereas the "second perfection" has to do with human redemption (the Incarnation) and the "final perfection" with the "perfect beatitude of the saints at the consummation of the world."[32] Since, in this final consummation humans are without material needs, animals and plants which are made for humans are no longer needed. "Therefore neither plants nor animals ought to remain."[33] Humans are graced, and will remain in the graced transformation of all, but the universe is natural and will only remain insofar as it pertains to humans. All

---

[30] See *Summa Theologica* 1.47.1.
[31] See Thomas Aquinas, *Compendium of Theology*, 148; quoted in Santmire, *Travail of Nature*, 91.
[32] See *Summa Theologica*, 1.73.1.
[33] See *Summa Theologica*, 3 Supp 91.5

is created good, but not everything will remain in glory. This is Thomas' legacy, and we will have to examine how Ignatius' view relates to it.

Before we compare Thomas with Francis of Assisi, let us mention Bonaventure (1217–1274) and Dante (1265–1321). Both followed Francis and were influenced by him, but both ultimately saw final fulfillment in humans rising above material creation. Bonaventure (unlike Thomas) wanted to include animals and plants in the state of glory, but had to argue that they are included in the human microcosm, not in themselves. The soul proceeds through creatures to God, but all nature is preserved only by participating in the human ascent.[34] Dante had a similar sense of God in all creation—like a divine poetry—but in the end humans had to leave the material to enter the inexpressible, immediate and imageless vision of God in triune glory. The divine hierarchy of Dionysius the Areopagite is again operative. The view of St. Francis is quite different.

Francis of Assisi: All Creation as God's Family

Francis (1181–1226) in many ways fulfilled the Celtic monk's ideal holy man—he befriended animals and tamed nature as Adam and Eve had done in paradise. Yet the reason behind what he

---

[34] See Leonard J. Bowman, "The Cosmic Exemplarism of Bonaventura," *Journal of Religion* 55 (1975) 195 [181–98]; Santmire, *Travail of Nature*, 102.

did was not a romantic idealization of nature, but a deep love of the Savior who emptied himself to care for lowly creatures. Thus, he is said to have cared for worms because the Savior said: "I am a worm and no man." Yet he did not just use the worm for a spiritual goal. He loved the worm, and as Celano says, "he used to pick them up in the way and put them in a safe place, that they might not be crushed by the feet of passers-by.[35] "He called by name of brother all animals, though in all their kinds the gentle were his favorites."[36] What Francis saw in nature was not Dante's Beatrice nor Alan Lille's goddess Natura, but Lady Poverty. His was a spirituality of *descent*, like the descent of the Son of God and God's love reaching to the lowliest of creatures. So he would call creatures to praise God, as in his sermon to the birds: "My little sisters, the birds, many are the bonds that unite us to God. And your duty is to praise Him everywhere and always ...."[37] Francis' mysticism was not so much a "nature mysticism" as a "Christ mysticism." In uniting with the self-emptying Savior, he also united

---

[35] See Thomas of Celano, *The First Life of St. Francis [1229] (Vita Prima)*, n. 61, in *St. Francis of Assisi: Writings and Early Biographies*, ed. Marion A. Habig (Chicago: Franciscan Herald, 1973) 225–55; Santmire, *Travail of Nature*, 109.

[36] See Celano, *The Second Life of St. Francis [1247] (Vita Secunda)*, n. 165: in *St. Francis of Assisi*, 357-543; Santmire, *Travail of Nature,* 109.

[37] See Celano, *Vita Prima*, n. 68f; Santmire, *Travail of Nature*, 110.

with the lowly animals and urged them to praise God for God's goodness.

Francis also had a strong eschatological consciousness. Yet, unlike Joachim of Fiore (1135–1202), his contemporary, it did not lead him to reject the church or sacraments in favor of an "Age of the Spirit." Francis remained intensely devoted to both church and sacraments. What he saw as the "last things" seemed to be expressed in his mysticism: "lion and lamb will lie down together with a child to lead them" (Isaiah 11:16). He lived the eschatological life already in this life, and welcomed death as a friend he had already gotten to know. His *Canticle*, indeed, was written after he had experienced the stigmata of Jesus, and was exhausted by sickness. He lived and died in solidarity with all the creatures of God. For him, they are not simply a means for humans to ascend to God, but are brothers and sisters who even now experience God's gracious care. Like Augustine, Francis sees God immediately involved with every creature, yet he expresses his vision in action whereas Augustine articulates it in writing.

Summary and Focus: A Resurrection Approach to the Environment

Developments after high scholasticism have not fundamentally changed this basic ambiguity with regard to the earth. Teilhard de Chardin felt it his life work to reintegrate spirituality with the earth, and he accomplished much toward this. But as Santmire points out, even Teilhard ends by subsuming all material creation in human transformation. As he writes: "In a convergent universe, every element finds its fulfillment, not directly in its own perfection, but in its incorporation into the unity of a superior pole of consciousness in which it can enter into communion with all others. Its worth culminates in a transmutation into the other, in a self-giving excentration"[38] Or again, "The end of the world: the overthrow of equilibrium, detaching the mind, fulfilled at last, from its material matrix, so that it will henceforth rest with all its weight in God's Omega."[39] These and other passages indicate that even Teilhard saw the universe as being subsumed in human fulfillment in Christ. Such a conclusion seems unwarranted, of course, given Teilhard's other presupposition that the preceding levels in evolution all remain in their own right even as they give rise to succeeding stages. Thus there seems no necessary reason to deny the inclusion of non-human creation in the final fulfillment.

Other approaches, such as the "Creation-centered Spirituality" of Matthew Fox and the "New Story" approach of Thomas Berry, so focus on the dynamics of creation that they downplay the need for redemption in Christ that is so cen-

---

[38] See Pierre Teilhard de Chardin, *The Future of Man*, trans. Norman Denny (New York: Harper & Row, 1959) 76.
[39] See Teilhard de Chardin, *The Phenomenon of Man*, trans. Bernard Wall (New York: Harper & Row, 1965) 287–88.

tral to the biblical message. Fox came to ground his approach in the work of Meister Eckhart and what he saw as a Fourfold Path of Spiritual Growth—Affirmation, Negation, Creativity, and Transformation. He is critical of St. Ignatius as leading to a kind of dualism (the type of separation of spirit and matter that we have noted in the tradition), even though he quotes with favor one scholar who says that Ignatius and Eckhart have basically the same position.[40] Ultimately, his (and Eckhart's) position is a kind of "realized eschatology," which itself is grounded in the redemptive resurrection of Christ, as key to a restored creation.

Thomas Berry has been inspired by Teilhard, but sees him as uncritical in not seeing the destructive effects of technology. Likewise, he distances himself from Teilhard's Christocentrism in favor of acknowledging the limited truth in every religious tradition. He would have us put away our Bibles for a good period of time in order to read the message of evolution, what he calls the "New Story." As he writes: "The universe itself, but especially the planet Earth, needs to be experienced as the primary mode of divine presence, just as it is the primary educator, primary healer,

---

[40] See Walter Nigg, *Warriors of God* (New York: Knopf, 1959) "Ignatian spirituality has much in common with that of Meister Eckhart; it is impossible, indeed, to approve the one while rejecting the other" (338). Quoted in Matthew Fox, *Breakthrough: Meister Eckhart's Creation Spirituality in New Translation* (Garden City, N.Y.: Doubleday, 1980) 2.

primary commercial establishment, and primary lawgiver for all that exists within this life community."[41] Unfortunately, creation does not explain itself or we would not need revelation. Nor does it redeem itself, or we would not need Jesus! We are left with an ambiguity similar to the tradition, only this time we are faced with an "either-or" of creation or redemption.

What is needed is a bridge between creation and redemption, a way to highlight the need for redemption (as Ignatius certainly does), but also bring creation and its transformation into that redemptive process. A view of resurrection as operative in our present life as well as in the future can help bridge this gap.[42] Through his resurrection Christ is made Lord of heaven and earth. All things are submitted to Christ that Christ can submit all to God that "God may be all in all" (1 Corinthians 15:28). This is clearly Ignatius' perspective, as we will see, as well as St. Francis'. The entire *Spiritual Exercises* is written in light

---

[41] See Thomas Berry, *The Dream of the Earth* (San Francisco: Sierra Club Books, 1990) 120.

[42] See Robert T. Sears, SJ, "Resurrection Spirituality and Healing the Earth," *Review for Religious* 49 (1990) 163–77. An expanded presentation is in Al Fritsch, SJ, and Robert T. Sears, SJ, *Earth Healing: A Resurrection-centered Approach* (privately published: ASPI, 1993). An excellent work based on the self-emptying love of the Trinity as seen in nature is Nancey Murphy and George F. R. Ellis, *On the Moral Nature of the Universe: Theology, Cosmology, and Ethics,* Theology and the Sciences (Minneapolis: Fortress, 1996). This is a carefully crafted "bottom up" and "top down" approach.

of Christ as "Eternal Lord of All Things" (Prayer for the Kingdom Meditation), as well as humble self-emptying servant. The split between human transformation and the redemption of creation seems to result from a separation of humans from the world (such as Thomas' view that humans were created in grace whereas creation was not) or an overly rationalized approach to the final transformation (like Origen's and even Teilhard's view). If the transformation is due to God's self-emptying and resurrecting love, and love preserves the otherness of the other and does not simply subsume it, then there would be no reason to deny a kind of self-emptying and resurrecting of the whole universe as the place where humans (and Christ as human) can contemplate in all its incarnate splendor, the immensity and diversity, beauty and harmony of God's creativity, as well as be immediately present to God. Such a view would lead us to be as passionately concerned about the earth and its healing as about humans, since humans and earth would be seen as united in God's love. Let us now look at the Exercises themselves to see how they would look on the environment from this resurrection-oriented approach of God's self-emptying love.

Chapter Two

The Environment in the Spiritual Exercises

IN the light of the historical survey in chapter 1, it is easy to see that Ignatius in the "Principle and Foundation" (and indeed in varying degrees throughout the *Spiritual Exercises*) was strongly influenced by the "ascent" approach to Christian spirituality. That is, he tended to see salvation as the human ascent to God through liberation from the allurements of this world. He did not, in other words, instinctively think of material creation as likewise participating with human beings in the Paschal Mystery, that is, in an ongoing spiritual rebirth to new life through identification with Christ in his passion, death and resurrection. Yet, as our reflections on the structure of the Exercises and on specific meditations within that overall structure in chapter 2 will make clear, there is in Ignatius' faith-vision the basis for an earth-centered (and resurrection-centered) approach to Christian spirituality. Admittedly, it only finds full expression in the "Contemplation to Attain Divine Love," but it is subtly at work in many of the key meditations of the Exercises.

Hence, while it would certainly be anachronistic to think of Ignatius as an early advocate of earth-centered spirituality, with proper qualifications the *Spiritual Exercises* can still be profitably used by directors and directees who have been sensitized to contemporary ecological concerns.

Principle and Foundation

In the "Principle and Foundation," for example, one notes the strongly anthropocentric and heavily individualistic tone of the opening sentences: "Human beings are created to praise, reverence and serve God our Lord, and by means of doing this to save their souls. The other things on the face of the earth are created for human beings to help them in the pursuit of the end for which they are created."[1] Ignatius was a man of his time, trained in scholastic philosophy and theology at the University of Paris. As a result, he was heavily task-oriented and somewhat rationalistic in his thinking. Yet as the "Contemplation to Attain Divine Love" makes clear, Ignatius was likewise sensitive to the beauty and inherent value of the world of non-human creation. Thus in explaining the "Principle and Foundation" one can legitimately direct the retreatant to a consideration of the role of humanity within the overall plan of creation. That would allow a fresh reading of

---

[1] Reference is to *The Spiritual Exercises of Saint Ignatius*, translated with a commentary by George E. Ganss, SJ (Chicago: Loyola University Press, 1992) n. 23. Hereafter: *SpEx*.

The Environment in the Spiritual Exercises

the celebrated "*Tantum-Quantum*" principle in the third sentence: "From this it follows that we ought to use these things to the extent that they help us toward our end, and free ourselves from them to the extent that they hinder us from it." Properly understood, this principle of *Tantum-Quantum* is an excellent strategy for an ecologically sensitive approach to material reality. For, while it overtly looks to the spiritual needs of the individual human being, it indirectly safeguards the rights of non-human creatures of God to live in relative peace and security within this world, safe from the spoliation of human beings bent on the satisfaction of their own ego-centered needs.

Non-human creatures, in other words, do not have to be urged to follow the principle of *Tantum-Quantum* in their dealings with one another. Lacking human self-awareness, they are not tempted to violate the rights of other creatures to life and well-being simply as a means to the satisfaction of their own narrowly conceived goals and values. Admittedly, there is often fierce competition for survival in the world of non-human nature with pain and loss of life as a necessary consequence. But animals do not add continually to their "survival-needs" as humans do to make their individual lives more comfortable and secure. Rather, they seem to observe instinctively the principle of *Tantum-Quantum* in the competition for survival in a world of limited resources. That is, they do not kill or victimize other animals simply for the sport of it but only to maintain their own place in the ecological "food-chain." Because they are, as noted above, lacking in human self-consciousness, they are not tempted to exaggerate their own importance within Nature's hierarchy and then to use violence to maintain it.

Human beings, on the other hand, are both blessed and cursed by the gift of self-awareness. Only because they are self-aware in a manner surpassing any other animal species, have human beings been able to use language to communicate with one another and to preserve the fruits of their individual and collective experience from one generation to another. In this way, various forms of human culture have gradually developed in different parts of the world. Likewise, in virtue of human self-awareness science and technology have arisen and dramatically altered the lifestyle of human beings, initially in the Western world, but increasingly now on a global scale. Anthropocentrism, accordingly, seems to be a regrettable but virtually inevitable byproduct of this meteoric rise of the human species to a position of pre-eminence among the living beings on the face of the earth. So much of the earth's resources is subject to human control that human beings are readily tempted to think that "the other things on the face of the earth" are indeed created solely for them to help them in attaining the goals and values which they themselves have chosen rather than, as Ignatius more cautiously puts it, in attaining the end for which they are created by God. Forgotten, then, is one's creaturehood as one attempts through heightened self-awareness to become master of one's fate and lord of the world within which one lives.

Ignatius, to be sure, in formulating the principle of the *Tantum-Quantum*, was unquestionably thinking in the first place of the individual's relationship to God as his or her Creator and Lord. But, insofar as he was thereby urging the retreatant to meditate on his or her creaturehood and the priority of God's intentions and to act accordingly, he was implicitly setting forth rules of behavior which would affect the relationship of human beings not only to God but likewise to one another and to the non-human world of creation as well. For, as we shall see below in greater detail, sin is basically a denial of one's creaturehood, a refusal to live in subordination to God and in proper co-ordination with other creatures who are also cared for by God. In seeking to "become like gods" (Genesis 3:5), human beings upset not only their relationship with God but likewise their natural relationship with all their fellow creatures. The harmony and well-being of the world order as originally intended by God are thus severely compromised with unnecessary suffering and loss of life as an inevitable consequence.

One other point needs to be stressed before moving on to a consideration of the meditations of the First Week from an ecological perspective. In a subsequent paragraph of the "Principle and

Foundation," Ignatius stresses the need for "indifference" to all created things. Here it would be easy to assume that indifference implies a lack of concern or care for others, even a lack of concern for one's own welfare, as Ignatius's dictum that one "ought not to seek health rather than sickness, wealth rather than poverty, honor rather than dishonor, a long life rather than a short one" might lead one to think. But this, it seems, would be a serious misrepresentation of what Ignatius really had in mind. For, true to his intent in the "Principle and Foundation" as a whole, Ignatius was simply stressing here the need to keep in mind one's creaturehood and the creaturely, that is, contingent, character of all the good things that this life can provide. They are not wrong in themselves provided that they are not chosen for the wrong reasons, that is, to shield oneself from the normal risks of creaturehood in a closely interdependent world. It may be, for example, that my efforts to guarantee health, riches, honor and a long life for myself will indirectly result in someone else not having the medical resources to sustain life or the economic resources to avoid grinding poverty and even starvation. My spiritual "indifference" to my own health and economic well-being, therefore, may well be necessary to give other human beings a chance for survival. For, in a world of limited resources, if some humans live in luxury, others will almost certainly live in poverty. Further, the real basis of "indifference" is a passionate desire to praise, reverence, and serve God, which implies an active care for the fullness of life for all God's creatures. For, if the triune God exhibits self-emptying love in the act of creation, then self-emptying love should be the norm, as far as possible, for our dealings with one another and all other sentient beings.

Similarly, in terms of Ignatius' principle, one might well question whether various non-human creatures (e.g., fur-bearing animals) should be exploited simply to make life more comfortable for those human beings who can afford a luxurious life-style. In each case, of course, an ethical decision must be made with respect to the good to be attained. But what Ignatius is recommending here is that one start this ethical deliberation from a position of genuine "indifference" to all created things rather than from a position of strong personal preference. Only then will one honestly assess one's true "needs" in a world of limited resources where hard choices frequently have to be made. In any event, Ignatian "indifference" does not mean lack of concern or care for others. Quite the contrary, the right kind of "indifference" generates strong feelings of compassion for one's fellow creatures. That is, as one progressively acknowledges with gratitude and love one's own creaturehood before God, one simultaneously experiences one's interdependence with other creatures within God's world. It is rather the de facto denial of one's creaturehood before God that leads to intense rivalry and conflict with one's fellow creatures in the competition to "become like gods" (Genesis 3:5), that is, to achieve one's personal security and well-being even at the cost of the security and well-being of others. As the Buddhist tradition has maintained for more than two thousand years now, wisdom leads to compassion. Knowledge of one's true place in the world allows one to make room for others, to give others likewise a fair chance for existence and well-being.

Meditations of the First Week

In the initial Exercise of the First Week, namely, that based on the history of sin, beginning with the sin of the angels, we have still another instance of the traditional "ascent" spirituality at work in Ignatius' mind and heart. In the "First Prelude" or the mental composition of place, for example, Ignatius proposes that the retreatant think of himself or herself "as imprisoned in this corruptible body" and as "an exile in this valley [of tears] among brute animals" (*SpEx*, n. 47). No more compelling testimony could be given to Ignatius' implicit belief that salvation is to be won through gradual emancipation from the things of this world. And yet it is interesting that in this as in all the other Exercises of the First Week, Ignatius calls attention to the corporate reality of sin and asks how I as an individual have escaped the just penalty of my sins. There is, in other words, an implicit awareness on Ignatius' part that the effects of sin move beyond the individual and eventually have cosmic significance. I as an individual am part of a corporate history of sin which began with the sin of the angels, was perpetuated with the sin of Adam and Eve, and is continued until the present day with the sins of individuals like myself. How is it that God has spared me even as God has allowed others to be condemned to hell for one sin or, in any case, for less sins than I have committed?

One should certainly not overestimate this insight of Ignatius into what we moderns today would call "sinful social structures," disordered behavior-patterns which were initiated by one group of human beings and subsequently perpetuated by countless others until the present day. His focus was clearly on the individual retreatant who needs to recognize with shame and confusion the disorder of his or her life. Yet for the contemporary retreat director or retreatant there is no reason why this initial Exercise of the First Week cannot be appropriately expanded to include explicit reflection on the social character of sin and one's own complicity in perpetuating "sinful social structures." The legitimation for this line of thought is implicit in Ignatius's own appeal to the history of sin as presented in the pages of Scripture. In each case, as noted above, sin is represented as a denial of one's creaturehood which is not only a denial of one's rightful subordination to God but also an implicit denial of one's interdependence with other creatures within the world order.

There is, to be sure, no reference to the impact of human sin on subhuman creation in this first Exercise. But in the second Exercise on one's personal sins there is clear reference to the way in which personal sin violates the order of non-human nature. In the third Point (*SpEx*, n. 58), for example, Ignatius urges the retreatant to compare himself or herself with all human beings, with the angels and saints in Paradise, with all of creation, and then ultimately with God as the author of creation. Then in the fifth Point (*SpEx*, n. 60) he asks why all these other creatures of God "have allowed me to live and have preserved me in life." Implicitly, therefore, Ignatius recognizes the social dimension of sin. My sins have a negative impact on all other creatures. Why do they not express their displeasure with me and conspire to send me to hell? Why do they instead continue to "serve" me even though by my sins I have not served them at all?

This last thought, to be sure, is an extrapolation from what Ignatius himself explicitly says. Given his heavily anthropocentric approach to creation, there is little reason to think that he likewise thought of human beings serving non-human nature (e.g., "the fruits, birds, fishes, and animals" of this world). But, once again, to a contemporary retreat director or retreatant who has been sensitized to ecological concerns and values, simply the image of an interconnected world of creatures presented by Ignatius here can surely inspire further reflection on how all God's creatures are meant to serve one another and how disordered human feelings and desires interfere with this "service" which creatures should render to one another as members of a common world.

Likewise, the cosmic dimension of Ignatius' thought comes to the fore in the colloquy for the meditation on hell where he asks the retreatant to divide the inhabitants of hell into three classes: "those lost before Christ came; those condemned during his lifetime; those lost after his life in this world" (*SpEx*, n. 71). In thus reflecting on salvation history as a whole, the retreatant should experience profound gratitude that he or she has not been numbered among one of these unfortunate groups of people. Once again, the principal focus of Ignatius is on the individual human being before God, but the overall context is that of salvation history as a whole in which human beings must bear corporate responsibility for the way in which events have taken place. No human being except Jesus and his mother is exempt from responsibility for the sins of this world. Hence, every human being alive today can express gratitude to God for thus far escaping the pains of hell. Circumstances of time and place more than one's own personal rectitude, it would seem, have within the loving providence of God given one the necessary "second chance" for salvation.

One could, of course, be critical here of Ignatius' "pessimistic" evaluation of human nature. But saints in all ages of the Church have expressed similar sentiments about the inherent weakness of human nature in the presence of temptation. Perhaps they alone have plumbed the depths of what it means to be a creature of God in a sinful world. On the one hand, they see unerringly the natural bent of human beings to make decisions in the light of their own narrow self-interest. On the other hand, they recognize that with God's grace they can live and act in line with the principle of *Tantum-Quantum* and thus serve both God and their neighbor with wisdom and compassion. In any event, even in these meditations of the First Week which are so strongly focused on the state of soul of the individual retreatant, Ignatius is aware of the full sweep of salvation history and of the corporate responsibility of human beings for the sorry state of affairs prevalent in human history up to now.

It is in this light that one should evaluate the famous colloquy to Christ on the cross at the end of the First Exercise where the retreatant is asked to reflect upon three questions: "What have I done for Christ? What am I doing for Christ? What ought I to do for Christ?" (*SpEx*, n. 53). Attention is here directed to Christ, not simply as an individual (even a divine-human individual), but as a symbol of a fallen world still capable of redemption. That is, Christ on the cross dramatically illustrates for the retreatant the ever-present reality of sin both in his or her personal life and in the surrounding world, and yet holds out to the retreatant the possibility of redemption, not only for himself or herself as an individual but for everyone and everything else in this world as well. In advance of the "Kingdom" meditation at the start of the Second Week, therefore, the appeal is to the common good over and above one's own personal desire for safety and well-being. Only thus will one effectively overcome the otherwise natural tendency to think once again in terms of one's own narrowly conceived self-interest and thus inevitably perpetuate the reign of sin both in one's own life and in the world at large.

Here too we must be careful not to claim too much by way of a cosmic perspective to Ignatius's thinking here. As a man of his time, he could not be expected to embrace consciously a creation-oriented spirituality which has become so popular in recent years with the development of ecological consciousness. But insofar as Ignatius in the "Principle and Foundation" and in these meditations of the First Week tried to draw the retreatant out of narrow preoccupation with his or her ego-centered goals and values, he left open the door for a contemporary retreat director or retreatant to introduce these further reflections on the interdependence of humans with other creatures of God in a world of limited resources.

The "Kingdom," after all, which Christ comes to proclaim, is not meant for humans alone but for all God's creatures. It is the reign of God in all of creation, not just in human salvation history. The focus in the colloquy with Christ on the cross in the First Week and in the "Kingdom" meditation is indeed on the struggle against the forces of evil in this world which have largely been generated by the sinful decisions of human beings. Hence, if the Kingdom is to be realized at all, it must be realized by human beings in the first place. Yet the effects of this spiritual renewal among humans will surely be felt in the world of non-human creation as well as in human history. As Paul comments in reflecting on life in the Spirit, "It was not for its own purposes that creation had frustration imposed on it, but for the purposes of him who imposed it—with the intention that the whole creation itself might be freed from its slavery to corruption and brought into the same glorious freedom as the children of God" (Rom 8:20-21). Human and non-human creation are linked in the divine plan of salvation.[2]

Call of the King and the Environment

Ignatius' Kingdom Meditation has been called a second foundation—a reflection that governs all that follows about Jesus' life and ministry. If we can understand its possible relation to the environment, we will have a key to all that follows. It also recapitulates the Foundation and the First Week, for it focuses the retreatant's desire to redress the harm done to God's creation in response

---

[2] See below, pp. 69–72, where a panentheistic model of the God-world relationship is outlined as a better way to understand how not just human beings but all of creation can be "saved," i.e., participate in the divine life.

to Christ whose cross and resurrection has freed one from sin and its effects. The question: "What have I done for Christ?" leads naturally to the self-offering for the work of Christ the King. Yet what is Christ's call, and what is its relevance for the environment?

To throw light on a possible link of the Call of the King to the environment it helps to recall: 1) that the King involved is our resurrected Lord who is fully divinized *in his humanity*, 2) that Ignatius was influenced by the lay "crusade spirituality" of his day, and 3) that Ignatius was a man of his time concerning the environment and saw it more in relation to God than to humans. The first point is clarified by Ignatius' Diary, which was found in his desk after his death.[3] In it is found a very strong focus on the persons of the Trinity and their one essence, and on the figure of Jesus in whom dwells "the Father, the Son, and the Holy Spirit, one only God, our Creator and Lord." Ignatius struggled during this time with how to reconcile the one essence of God and the three persons. Then on Feb. 21, 1544, this "knot" was resolved at his Mass. "I recognized, felt, or saw, the Lord knows, that in speaking to the Father, and in seeing that He was a Person of the most Holy Trinity, I was moved to love the Trinity all the more since the other Persons

---

[3] See Adolf Haas, "The Mysticism of St. Ignatius according to His Spiritual Diary," in *Ignatius of Loyola: His Personality and Spiritual Heritage, 1556–1956*, ed. Friedrick Wulf (St. Louis: Institute of Jesuit Sources, 1977) 164–99.

were present in it essentially (*essencialmente*). I felt the same in the prayer to the Son, and the same in the prayer to the Holy Spirit, rejoicing in each one of them and feeling consolation. And attributing this to all Three, I was filled with joy because I belonged to all Three and thus the 'knot' was solved."[4] So also, even when his devotions "terminated in Jesus" he saw Jesus as "Son of the Father" and cried out in the Spirit "What a Father, what a Son!" [72]. Ignatius experienced the divine "circumincession," the total self-giving and indwelling of the divine Persons in one another, and this gave him intense joy.

Similarly, the human Jesus is "totally God" [87], the dwelling-place of the most Holy Trinity. Jesus is totally divinized even in the smallest and apparently least significant fact of his historical existence including his death. Through Christ the return of the world to the triune God becomes possible, and Mary is the gateway to Christ. In Jesus, the divinity of the Triune God enters into the very depths of creation in order to bring all creation into the unity of God's life. This mystery of transformation was experienced especially during the Eucharist—its preparation, actual celebration and the thanksgiving that permeated the rest of the day for Ignatius. In it the self-emptying love of God for the world

---

[4] Ibid., 178; Spiritual Diary, [63]. Henceforth quotations will be taken from the Spiritual Diary in *Ignatius of Loyola: Spiritual Exercises and Selected Works*, ed. George E. Ganss, SJ (New York: Paulist, 1991) 235–70.

was enacted. Thus, Ignatius' desire "to seek and find God in all things" Haas sees as focused on Christ. Ignatius speaks of Christ as "Creator and Lord crucified for [our salvation]."[5] The final vow formula has the vows made to "Almighty God in the presence of His Virgin Mother."[6] Christ enters very concretely into creation as we see from the minute details of the Incarnation and Nativity Contemplations, and he fulfils his call in his total self-gift on the cross. This explains why Ignatius wanted first to go to the very land of Jesus—Jerusalem—to serve him, and why, when that proved impossible, he bound himself instead by vow to the concrete embodiment of Christ on earth, the Pope as visible center of the Catholic Church as Body of Christ. His mystical vision saw Christ as the eternal mediation of God with creation—"Eternal Lord of All Things," as he says in the offering of the Kingdom meditation. Thus, the Call of the King is a mystical vision, the call of our crucified and resurrected "Creator and Lord" to become coworkers for the return of all things to God.

Secondly, Ignatius' view was influenced, it seems clear, by the lay crusade spirituality of his day.[7] Ignatius was a layman for most of the pe-

---

[5] *The Constitutions of the Society of Jesus and Their Complementary Norms* (St. Louis: Institute of Jesuit Sources, 1996): First and General Examen, n. 66 (p. 37).

[6] Ibid.: Constitutions, n. 532 (p. 206).

[7] See Hans Wolter, "Elements of Crusade Spirituality in St. Ignatius," in *Ignatius of Loyola: His Personality and Spiritual*

riod of his formation. In order to understand his perspective we need to understand the dominant spirituality of his time, the crusader spirit. The crusader "took the Cross and made his vow because he believed that God was calling him. He perceived the voice of God in the admonitions of the popes, the preachers, and of his bishop. The will of the divine Lord—and it was a question of recapturing His earthly home, of protecting His faithful, of extending His kingdom—was for the crusaders an inescapable duty." The crusade, whatever we may think of it today, was then "a participation in the work of Christ." The crusader was drafted into the army of Christ, placed under Christ's command. Yet in a deeper sense, the crusade was "a following of Christ." The exertions and sufferings and possible death were all taken into consideration as a "spiritual participation in the suffering and death of Christ. Beyond that, victory—granted but seldom—was experienced as a participation in the victory of Christ and the glorification of Christ."[8] Christ was universal King, and it was because Christ's homeland (the Holy Land) was "a type of the *universa terra*, the whole world, that the Reconquest of Spain [from the Moors] and the conquest of the New World for Christianity were seen as equivalent to the conquest of Palestine. The *terra sancta* and the

---

Heritage, 1556–1956: Studies on the 400th Anniversary of His Death, edited by Friedrich Wulf (St. Louis: Institute of Jesuit Resources, 1977) 97–134.

[8] Ibid., 109; Spiritual Diary, [63].

The Environment in the Spiritual Exercises

whole earth belong together in the same way that mid-point and circumference constitute one circle." Hence the desire of Ignatius (like St. Francis before him) was to win the Holy Land for Christ, and he committed himself to serve the vicar of Christ to win the whole earth when that became impossible. His was no merely spiritual service. Even service in hospitals (which was an integral part of the crusader spirit, and of the military orders of that time), was a concrete service of the homeless Christ. And part of the spirituality of the crusade was that "all fought together," and even those at home helped by interceding for those who fought. This view of many intercessors also became an integral part of Ignatian spirituality. Ignatius "the pilgrim" was always on a journey to the "Holy Land," in service of Christ's church, to attain the redemption of all creation for its Creator and Lord—Christ.

Thirdly, however, creation, for Ignatius, was not the evolving scientific universe we now presuppose. It was a Ptolemaic universe, as Toolan reminded us, that was more linked to God than humans. Nowhere that we know of does Ignatius hint that creation needs redemption. It is humans that are the object of Christ's Call "to win the world." Creation is on God's side, and in the First Week we are to wonder: "the heavens, sun, moon, stars, and the elements; the fruits, birds, fishes, and other animals—why have they all been at my service!" There is biblical warrant for this view in the Noah covenant where God would no longer destroy the earth because of human sin. The Land is God's "promise" when we turn back to God. Yet we live with the awareness that our self-serving use of technology can indeed kill creation. Does that not mean that our Call to save humans includes saving the Earth, as well as letting the Earth reveal God to us? How can humans be "saved"—that is, brought into line with God's will—without changing their attitude toward creation and serving God's intentions for creation? We need to become aware that creation is both a revelation of God's grace (it reveals our sin and offers us life) and is itself in need of redemption. At base, does it not "share" in the self-emptying of God by "serving us"? Does it not call forth our self-giving "service" in response to God?

In any case, Ignatius' view of the earth, while not being "creation-centered" (it is rather "Christ-centered" or better "God-centered"), is nevertheless permeated by Christ's Spirit and reveals God's gracious presence. Humans are called to an active coworking with God to "serve" God's intentions for the world (the cosmos, we would now say). This is not simply a spiritual call. Ignatius mystically saw all creation proceeding from the Triune God and through the Incarnation being brought back to God. In "winning all people to Christ" whose healing involves our environment, our call is also to rescue the environment—the *terra sancta* of the whole world—from all Christ's enemies (or self-centered social powers) and bring it back to the service of God's love. That this will have to be through the conversion of humans seems clear, but the saving of the Earth can also be one way of bringing humans to an awareness of a larger goal than their own narrow interests. For finding God in creation opens us to a reverence for all creatures. Then our willingness "to bear all wrongs and all abuse and all poverty, both actual and spiritual" (*SpEx*, n. 98) will be focused concretely on activating the Spirit of Christ's self-giving love in this very wounded earth. The goal is "God's Greater Glory", by freeing humans and the earth from its present exploitation to the fullness of mutual self-gift that God intends for it.

The King's Way as Our Way: Incarnation and Nativity

Ignatius looks on the Incarnation and Birth of Jesus as "models for all the other contemplations."[9] We are to enter concretely into the actual life of Jesus which is also a revelation of God in human life. The exercitant "with the inner eyes of the soul" is to see the road from Nazareth to Bethlehem, to see the size of the cave, and to be a servant who with great reverence tries to see the holy persons, etc. The mystery is to become concretely part of one's own history, and through felt contact with Jesus one is permeated with "the infinite fragrance and sweetness of the Divinity." This very concrete and direct experience and de-

---

[9] See Haas, "The Mysticism of St. Ignatius," 188.

sire to imitate Jesus is what makes Ignatius want to realize his goal at first in the Holy Land itself, and later in submission to the Vicar of Christ, for making the whole world God's land. Each contemplation, like the Mass, is an encounter with a unique, historical event that has universal and divine implications. In the uniqueness of Christ's life, and by implication, the uniqueness of every creature of God, God's love and presence is enacted.

The Incarnation meditation takes us concretely to the divine side of this total mystery. Here the retreatant is with the three persons of the Trinity (as Ignatius continued to be throughout his life as we saw from his Diary). The beauty of the Trinity's perfect sharing and presence to one another in their essential unity had moved Ignatius to tears for a whole day, and moved him powerfully in his Manresa period. With the Trinity the retreatant is to look out over "the face of the earth" to see the different races and peoples "in great blindness, going down to death and descending into Hell"(*SpEx*, n. 106). The focus is on the people, not the earth itself for the earth is indwelt by God; but Ignatius' vision embraces the earth in all its concreteness. The retreatant is to "hear what they say"—in order to understand humans and the divine intention in their regard: how the people speak to each other, "swear and blaspheme", and how the divine persons say "let us work the redemption of the human race" and how the angel speaks to Mary. Finally the retreatant is to "see what they do"—which opens us to human and divine actions. How people "wound and kill and go down to Hell" and how the divine persons "work the most holy Incarnation" and "how our Lady humbles herself, and offers thanks to the divine Majesty." We then are to reverently enter into dialogue with the figures in the contemplation. We are to speak to the "Three Divine Persons," or to the "Eternal Word Incarnate," or "His Mother, Our Lady" and ask for the grace to follow and imitate more closely our Lord in his redemptive mission.

This Ignatian perspective, familiar to every Jesuit, shows clearly that Ignatius views humans as fallen and in need of being brought back to God. Creation is here not so much a way to find God as a place in which to work with God for redemption. Though the earth itself is not spoken of (Ignatius' focus is ever on human salvation), it seems reasonably clear what his view would be if he had taken the earth into consideration. It is God's creation and it is being brought back to God through the Incarnation. If it shares in the effects and the sinfulness of humans, as we now clearly see in its exploitation and "crucifixion" by humans, it also needs to be drawn into God's life and brought "back to God" through Jesus' Incarnation. We cannot neglect Mary's role in this process. She is central to Ignatius' view. With Jesus she is our God-given, universal intercessor and model of cooperation with God's redemptive initiatives. Her very flesh was also that of her

Son.[10] She is, as it were, the heart of the earth saying "Yes" to its redemption, the recreation of its "glory" as God's dwelling, the "eternal feminine" (in Teilhard's words) that delights in God and from the heart of the earth buds forth the savior. She is the model of self-emptying love as she painfully says "Yes" to Christ's painful self-giving on the cross. It is not by accident that the ecological movement and the activation of the feminine are emerging together. Mary's "humble reception" models the humility that Ignatius sees as central to our opening to the self-revelation of God in the person of Jesus.

When we move to the Nativity meditation, we see more clearly how Ignatius views this co-working with God. There we see Mary and Joseph "and the maid" (a "servant" that Ignatius includes from Ludolf's presentation of the mysteries) obeying the edict of Caesar (God using even secular rulers and events) and going to the cave in Bethlehem (a place close to the earth and animal life), and the child Jesus being born there. We hear what they say (nothing is suggested) and see what they do—"making the journey and laboring that our Lord might be born in extreme poverty, and that after many labors, after hunger, thirst, heat, and cold, after insults and outrages, He might die on the cross, and all this for me." (*SpEx*, n. 116) Ignatius views Jesus' birth as the

---

[10] See Spiritual Diary [31], quoted in Haas, "The Mysticism of St. Ignatius," 187.

The Environment in the Spiritual Exercises

beginning of a long pilgrimage to work out our redemption. We glimpse already Ignatius' "crusade spirituality" at work to release humans and all creation from captivity to sin. Its heart is "extreme poverty" that frees the retreatant from possessing and being possessed by created things in order to be grounded in the Creator and Lord of All Things, so as to "find God in all things." Ignatius' "ascent spirituality" (being purified from attachment to all things so as to unite fully with God) is here linked with a "descent spirituality"—namely, with God to embrace all things in order to draw them back to God. It is an active self-emptying, a spirituality that dies to self for God and thereby brings the world into God's ever new life.

In the succeeding meditations (the Presentation, the Flight to Egypt, the Obedience of Jesus to his parents, and the Finding in the Temple), Ignatius shows the conflict—"the fall and the rise of many"—that Jesus' mission will cause, and how it relives Israel's persecution and liberation from Egypt. Yet he also includes Jesus' hidden life, how he "learned" from his parents and his tradition at the same time that he sought only God as ground of his call (Luke 2:41-50 "Finding in the Temple") and how he "grew in wisdom, age, and grace" (Luke 2:51-52). Ignatius mentions his carpenter trade (*SpEx*, n. 271), but we today might also consider how at this time he grew in love of creation and saw God's teaching in "the wild flowers," "birds" and "sun shining on good and bad alike." Jesus learned about his Father from nature. Ignatius saw God's teaching in creation just as his master did. Contemplating the stars inspired him with a desire to serve Our Lord (*Autobiography*, n. 11). Creation belongs to God ("The land is mine," Lev 25:23) and as we grow in reverence for it, we learn how God teaches us through it, even through its devastation which, like Jesus' cross, reveals our sin. This can open us to a more active response in light of Jesus' public life.

Christ's Public Life and the Ignatian Strategy

What Ignatius noted in passing in the Kingdom and Nativity meditations, he makes an explicit criterion for discernment in the Two Standards—that God directs the soul through poverty and humility—God's self-emptying love.[11] The Two Standards also shows most clearly how the spiritual life is seen by Ignatius as a kind of crusade, a battle to regain creation for Christ. There are two fronts, an outer and an inner front. There are

---

[11] Donald W. Mitchell, *Spirituality and Emptiness: The Dynamics of Spiritual Life in Buddhism and Christianity* (New York: Paulist, 1991), shows how our deep self-emptying opens us to solidarity with all beings and releases a deep compassionate love. What the Exercises do is ground that important dynamic in the person of Jesus and God's trinitarian self-emptying love. See also Nancey Murphy and George F. R. Ellis, *On the Moral Nature of the Universe*, for an argument that God's self-emptying love is the ground or vital source of the laws of the cosmos and of human social reality.

The Environment in the Spiritual Exercises

two banners and two armies: the banner of Satan and his army, sent to every person and place, and the banner of Christ and his army. Here, it is not a question of who one will follow. That was the focus of the Kingdom meditation. Here, it is a question of strategy. As Howard Gray, SJ, points out in his retreat on the Exercises, many want to serve Christ, but few want to use his strategy!

What is Christ's strategy in the concrete, and how does it relate to the environment? It is a divine, not human strategy. The strategy of Lucifer (the "light-bearer") rests more on human power. It originates (and terminates) in Babylon—the city (spoken of by Augustine in the City of God) which springs from the confusion and pride of the tower of Babel—and is spread to the whole world. It entices people to possessions, prestige and power, no doubt to do "good things," not unlike Jesus' temptations after his Baptism. From there it is a short step to becoming enamored of one's own ideas and control. All sorts of divisiveness and destructiveness can then result—from the blatant exploitation of multinational corporations to the more hidden internecine warfare and lack of unity in "Christian" institutions.

The strategy of Christ our Lord originates in Jerusalem—the city of peace. His "sacred doctrine" (God's "holy strategy") is just the opposite! He lures His followers to delight in poverty and detachment so that God will be one's total security, much as Jesus rebuked his tempter: "humans do not live on bread alone, but on every word of

God" (Matthew 4:4). This is to lead to detachment from recognition and prestige—much as Jesus remained focused on God both when the crowds idolized him for his miracles and when they abandoned him as he spoke of his passion. It leads to the humility of total trust in God and desire for God's glory. Poverty, for Ignatius, was not for individual asceticism. He sought the poverty of the crusader, one who sacrifices everything and perhaps even his life to follow Jesus in His campaign. But more deeply, it was the poverty of God, the essential self-emptying of the divine persons for each other and for humankind that had brought him to tears. That poverty and humility lead to a reverent oneness with the poor earth and its creatures and to a oneness with other human beings and with God. The true God is humble. "Learn of *me*," Jesus says, "for I am meek and humble of heart" (Matthew 11:29). And it is the meek who will "inherit the land" (Matthew 5:5; Psalm 37:11, 22). God empties self to be in loving solidarity with the least and most abandoned creatures, and calls each to a similar free response of love.

Ignatius' understanding of Christ's strategy is very much like the example of St. Francis, only with a more activist drive to it.[12] Francis' focus on

---

[12] Francis always felt a kinship with creation. Even before his conversion he delighted in nature. But it was his leaving his father's riches and his growing love for Jesus and the self-emptying poverty of the humble Son of God that brought him into his deepest communion with nature. Lady Poverty became

poverty was very timely as a God-given response to the rise of commercialism and the growing intellectual "riches" of the Church.[13] Poverty is what united Francis and Ignatius to the poor Christ and awakened a deep gratitude and reverence for all things as gifts of God's self-emptying love. Far from leading us to "dominate" creation (as some have wrongly interpreted Gen 1:28), this "strategy" would lead us to reverence other creatures and selflessly care for their needs as God cares for us. This might look "stupid and ineffectual" to a more politically inclined view (the "dishonor" that would likely result), but it would release a power greater than every other power—the power of love.

---

his bride, his way, not as an ideology, but because that was the way of Jesus. This very poverty brought him into deep solidarity with all creatures. As already mentioned, his *Canticle of Brother Sun* was written shortly before his death after he had received the stigmata. Thus the utmost poverty fueled the greatest praise of God and delight in all God's least creatures, just as for Ignatius the greater his poverty, the greater his gratitude and love of God's gracious kindness in all things.

[13] See Mario von Galli, SJ, *Living Our Future: Francis of Assisi and the Church Tomorrow* (Chicago: Franciscan Herald, 1972), chapter 4, where he notes how Vatican II was confronted with the challenge of "poverty" and becoming the Church of Jesus by becoming the church of the poor. However, it chose not to include that view in its documents. It was presumably too much of a challenge. Ignatius had the same appreciation of poverty as Francis, and the same desire for institutional poverty as well as for poverty on the part of individuals. He saw the same spiritual dangers in the acquisition of riches, but his followers like those of Francis did not sustain that ideal. The challenge remains today.

This strategy is so important, and so difficult to attain or even understand, that Ignatius adds two other reflections to make us aware of the level of our commitment to it—the Three Classes of Men and the Three Degrees of Humility. The Three Classes meditation tests our willingness really to detach ourselves from possessions (how central our desire and choice of poverty truly is). It brings the meditation on the Two Standards into one's concrete, embodied life. If the thousand ducats symbolize one's use of material goods, how free would one be to let go of attachment to them in order to serve God's intentions? Has the desire for control and narrow self-interest subtly taken over our lives? Have we yielded to the lure of a more affluent way of life or the desire for financial security? Do we instead have the deep sense of gratitude for the gift of life, however it is presented to us? Which Spirit governs my actual life is the question Ignatius puts here to the retreatant. The Contemplations on Jesus' Public Life are to deepen this awareness and lead to a total commitment to Jesus' own way of life, his deep trust in God's care for him even as he felt increasingly powerless before enemies intent on killing him.

The Three Degrees of Humility is a reflection to be done before the Election—the choice of how one is to lead one's life in imitation of Christ. Ignatius focuses on the Third Degree, presupposing that the first and second were already considered through reflection on the Three

The Environment in the Spiritual Exercises

Classes of Men: "Whenever the praise and glory of the Divine Majesty would be equally served, in order to imitate and be in reality more like Christ our Lord, I desire and choose poverty with Christ poor, rather than riches; insults with Christ loaded with them, rather than honors; I desire to be accounted as worthless and a fool for Christ, rather than to be esteemed as wise and prudent in this world. So Christ was treated before me." (*SpEx*, n. 167). Our love for Christ is to make us prefer His way of poverty, humiliations and humility. "For has not God made foolish the wisdom of the world?" (1 Corinthians 1:20). "The foolishness of God is wiser than men, and the weakness of God is stronger than men." (1 Corinthians 1:25). The world's "wisdom" leads to pride and competition and blatant disregard of the needs of others, whereas the "foolishness" of Jesus' way leads to love and reverence for all God's creatures, both human and non-human, especially those least able to fend for themselves against overt human aggression.

Granted that the mysteries of Christ's Public Life are to be contemplated in the light of the Two Standards, what effect will opting for Jesus' way have on one's approach to the environment? Little is said directly but much is implied. The Beatitudes focus on poverty of spirit and on the "meek who will inherit the land," seeking God's way and becoming peacemakers. Whereas the covetous "store into barns," those that follow Jesus "store up treasure in heaven" (Luke 12:13-

21). They know that God clothes the grass of the fields without human worry or toil. But Ignatius also includes mysteries where Jesus more actively assumes authority over creation: the multiplication of the loaves and the calming of the sea. Jesus' poverty and openness to God really does open Him to "God's rule," as He "commands the storm and the sea and it obeys him" (Matthew 8:23-27; *SpEx*, n. 279). The authority over nature originally given to Adam is restored in Jesus that nature might serve God's plan. Jesus even performs the deep miracles of God's creative power to give life such as in the raising of Lazarus (John 11). Curiously, Ignatius does not include the healing of the man born blind (John 9), whereas that healing teaches that suffering is also involved in witnessing to Christ. The deeper the revelation of God's power in Christ, the greater the opposition from the dominant powers of his day. The more people followed him (as with the raising of Lazarus and triumphant entry into Jerusalem), the greater the opposition to him and plot on his life. It would seem that those who stand up for the poor and the powerless, including the earth as powerless, can expect nothing different.

The Election

For Ignatius, it is not enough simply to understand God's way of self-emptying love. We need to choose accordingly and to live by that choice. We give God our memory, understanding and

The Environment in the Spiritual Exercises

will (the *Suscipe*). Our primary choice is to be united to Christ in his redemptive work. But the retreatant is also to choose what state of life is most conducive to that choice, or within one's given state of life, how one should reform one's life to be more in accord with God's Spirit (see *SpEx*, n. 189 on the "Reformation of One's Way of Living"). Christ's way of life touches every detail: "how large a household he should maintain, how he ought to rule and govern it . . . how much should be set aside for distribution to the poor and other pious purposes. . . . [H]is progress will be in proportion to his surrender of self-love and of his own will and interests." The retreatant "finds" God by living ever more in accord with God's Spirit. This directive should affect each retreatant's personal approach to the environment as well. But it is also a directive for institutions. Reinhold Niebuhr argued many years ago that it is even more difficult for institutions to live a selfless life than it is for individuals, since it can seem "selfless" for individuals to sacrifice for the institution, whereas the institution can be unconsciously quite "self-centered" while thinking it is serving God.[14] Ignatius' Diary is a reflection

---

[14] See Reinhold Niebuhr, *Moral Man and Immoral Society: A Study in Ethics and Politics* (New York: Scribner, 1932). Murphy and Ellis (*On the Moral Nature of the Universe*) questioned Niebuhr's generalizations about institutions not being able to exist selflessly. From their Anabaptist perspective, nonviolence can also function as an institutional strategy. But, given his many historical examples of institutional self-centeredness, Niebuhr's argument still challenges us.

on the poverty proper to houses of the Society of Jesus, not just each Jesuit's personal poverty. If we all lived the poverty and simplicity of Jesus' life, what choices would we need to make to care for the environment as God does? As we enter into solidarity with the world of plants and animals as well as the human world, what selfless decisions should we make for their best interests as well as our own, and for God's glory in all creation? What sacrifices need to be made? What interventions on behalf of the poor earth?

The Passion: In Labor with God

Decisions have implications when carried out, and will involve suffering and perhaps even death in confrontation with self-centered forces that oppose God's way. This is especially true if we are called to confront social injustice or exploitation. Yet the power Jesus relied on (and on which we are to rely) is not primarily political power (though Ignatius was an astute politician for God's interests) but God's self-emptying love. Paradoxically, that power works through our "weakness" and our ability to persevere with faith in God's love despite suffering and even death. We need "great effort" (*SpEx*, n. 195) to enter into the grief and sadness of Jesus as he struggles to stay united with God's love while confronting the sin of the world. The Cross is the ultimate mystery of God's self-emptying love confronting human powers. Rejection of the cross is

The Environment in the Spiritual Exercises

the ultimate sign of the demonic. Peter recoiled when Jesus foretold his passion, but Jesus replied "Get behind me Satan! You are not on the side of God but of humans" (Mark 8:33) And under the cross he was taunted "Let him come down now from the cross and we will believe in him" (Matt 27:42). The belief that Christ is Son of God, works miracles, reveals a new way of life—all this is acceptable to the modern view. After all, we humans work miracles with nature through science, and even New Agers believe they are one with the divine and that somehow nature is divine. But that God personally "dies on the cross for us," and that we also must die for Him and for one another (and the earth)—that is the ultimate challenge to our human nature and to our view of who God is. Yet paradoxically, what seems like defeat is a victory over death that frees us from the fear of failure, rejection and suffering that makes us exploit one another and the earth so as to make our own lives secure. Not trusting God, we (individuals and institutions) take over God's role for ourselves and for the earth. Power replaces self-emptying love. The more power, the less love. On the other hand, the more love, the more respect for freedom, not just for humans but for all creation (Rom 8:21). God's love is the vital source of all that exists, but sin clouds that truth. Hence the challenge is to stay rooted in trust of God's love despite the attacks of deeply embedded human and Satanic powers that have exploited creation for self-serving ends. "This is the victory that overcomes the world, our faith" (1 John 5:4).

The challenge to get free of individual and institutional self-centeredness in order to be rooted in God's love is what Ignatius places before us from the First Week to the end of the Exercises. Now, in the Passion, we are to be grounded in pure faith in God, with all other supports being removed. We are to consider how "the divinity hides itself . . . it could destroy its enemies and does not do so." We are to consider "what Christ our Lord suffers in His human nature . . . or what he desires to suffer" (Jesus' deliberate choice). And finally, we consider that "Christ suffers all this for my sins, and what I ought to do and suffer for Him" (we take responsibility for our sins, and our part in the sin of the world). As Jesus was drawn into the sin of the world he experienced a strong sense of God's absence as he cried out, "My God why have you abandoned me?" (Mark 15:34). This is not just his own scream but the "primal scream" of humanity—the effect of our sin of abandoning God which is buried in humanity's collective unconscious. Did he not then also experience the cry of the earth for deliverance into the "freedom of the children of God"? Is the earth itself not like an abandoned child whose parents have lost their relation to God and are absorbed in their own interests, either idolizing the child or totally neglecting it? What does it mean that "the whole creation has been groaning in travail . . . as we wait for the glorious free-

The Environment in the Spiritual Exercises

dom of the children of God" (Romans 8:18-25)? Christ's dying releases new divine life. As we die in Christ we touch that mystery of new life. We experience God's self-giving love (the opposite of Satan's power) as the key to the very life of creation. With non-human creation, this surrender to the life of the whole is its natural dynamic. With humans, it must be freely chosen so as to resist the self-assertion of the sinful powers of this world within consciousness. The struggle begins in the heart of every individual, but it also reaches into the heart of humanity as a whole and of creation.

The various mysteries of the Passion open up the fullness of this truth. In the Last Supper Jesus gives his body and blood for the life of the world, showing that material creation now has a new grounding in the Incarnate Lord. As Teilhard de Chardin experienced it, the whole world is offered up in Jesus and given back as divine communion. Each aspect of creation is opened, through sharing Christ's death (to self-enclosedness) and resurrection, so as to feed and nourish us with God's presence. "Unless the grain die, it remains alone, but if it dies, it bears much fruit" (John 12:24). In his Agony, Jesus labors to stay true to God's will and to keep faith in God's unbreakable love by taking on himself the implications of the sin of the world. In each mystery, he "wants to suffer" what each of us suffers in order to move us beyond our fear of death, lostness, and despair and to trust in God. His scourging and condemnation is the image of many prisoners today. His being bound and nailed to the cross is what many sick experience. And his dying with forgiveness has brought healing to many relationships and families. For, through his passion and death, he founded a new community of compassion symbolized by the way he gave "his mother and beloved disciple" to one another in his dying moments (John 19:26-27).[15]

The Resurrection

Even though the Passion and Resurrection are experienced as quite distinct, in reality they are two aspects of a single mystery. The passion is the glorification of Jesus, according to John. It is his consecration in the Truth, his final manifestation of the Glory of God. Yet in the resurrection Jesus' divinity is revealed, not concealed as in his passion, and he is empowered "to console" (*SpEx*, nn. 223–24). As Jesus "desired to suffer" in the Third Week, now he performs the office of consoler—the office credited to the Holy Spirit. When we share in this aspect of his mystery, we also are empowered to console, to heal, to reconcile, to manifest the compassion of God. Every resurrection apparition involves a "sending"! We are sent to be part of the transforming mission of

---

[15] Over the centuries many Christians have found comfort and new strength in dealing both with their own sufferings and with the sufferings of those for whom they care through contemplation of the suffering of Jesus in the passion narratives. Compassion, after all, is learning how to suffer for and with others.

The Environment in the Spiritual Exercises

Jesus, to bring all into submission to Christ, that Christ may submit all to God the Father, that God may be all in all (1 Corinthians 15:28).

The resurrection mysteries show the various ways consolation is brought and people are commissioned. Is there some relation to the environment that can be glimpsed in them? Ignatius has Jesus appear first to his mother.[16] She is empowered now to "mother" the "total Christ" (including the earth?).[17] Mary Magdalene is encountered in the garden. Her love is moved from "clinging" (being focused on the physical presence of Jesus) to being "sent" to the disciples—from the individual Christ to the "Total Christ" (as Augustine said). The garden of the fall is transformed into a garden of renewed communion. The two disciples going to Emmaus (who symbolize early Christians disillusioned by suffering) are helped

---

[16] Gilles Cusson lists some twenty writers who have held this opinion including St. Teresa of Avila. See his *Biblical Theology and the Spiritual Exercises* (St. Louis: Institute of Jesuit Studies, 1994) 303–4.

[17] Some years ago, I (Bob Sears) experienced in a retreat how Jesus could reveal the full mystery of his human/divine being to Mary. This "first" apparition was really a foundational apparition, for Mary alone was fully able to receive the full meaning of Jesus' life, death, and resurrection. She had been intimately part of his life from his conception to agony on the cross! He was flesh of her flesh (as Ignatius saw). I could appreciate how John had such a mystical universal vision if he lived with Mary. As Mary fully receives Jesus' life she becomes the spiritual mother of all, for she embodies the fullness of what we are to grow into. Is Mary not the spiritual mother of the earth as well as all Christians, for it also is Christ's Body?

by Jesus to see hope in their suffering, and finally to recognize him in the "breaking of the bread!" They can perceive his bodily presence only through accepting their own suffering, and their joy brings them back to community. The disciples meet Jesus in the upper room. He breathes the Spirit on them, grounding a new creation, and sends them out with a ministry of reconciliation! When Thomas encounters Jesus a week later he must touch Jesus bodily. Jesus is not a disembodied spirit, but still incarnate even as a risen person. When he encounters the disciples by the sea, he again uses nature to reveal God's truth as they are told where to catch the boatload of fish. The commission to Peter to "feed my lambs" does not mention the earth, but Jesus' prior feeding of the disciples with bread and fish shows that his commision is not purely spiritual but also material. Embodied persons are to be nourished by a renewed earth. Jesus' final commission to the five hundred in Galilee is to go into the whole world, teaching them to observe all that he had commanded (Matthew 28:20). He will be with them all days to the end of time. Nothing is said about nature in Matthew's account of that final moment, though in Mark's narrative (Mark 16:17-18) Jesus predicts that miracles will accompany the disciples' preaching of the Gospel.

Does the material and animal creation also experience the resurrection? Some, like Aquinas, held that only humans were created in grace and only humans would experience final transforma-

The Environment in the Spiritual Exercises

tion. Others, like Irenaeus and Augustine and it seems St. Francis, said that all creation does and will experience resurrection. It is difficult to say where Ignatius stood on this issue since he never spoke directly to it, and he seemed to focus Christ's mission on human salvation. Yet several reasons argue that had he considered this issue, he would have included all creation in the effects of the resurrection.

In the first place, Ignatius was touched by God in creation. It is commonly known that he used to sit on his roof to watch the stars since they filled him with a desire to do great things for God. Or he could be moved to tears at the sight of a flower: "If this flower is already so lovely, how lovely then must be the Lord."[18] Secondly, he saw this same creation springing from the Creator, but also penetrated by the humanity of Christ and being brought back to God through Christ. It was the resurrected Christ, our Creator and Lord, that was always in the center of his thoughts. His goal was "to seek God in all things . . . loving Him in all creatures and all creatures in Him."[19] He did not let creation become our focus, but his discovery of God was not separate from creation but in and through all creatures. Since all creation reveals to humans the infinite

---

[18] See Lambert Classen, "'The 'Exercise with the Three Powers of the Soul' in the Exercises as a Whole," in *Ignatius of Loyola: His Personality and Spiritual Heritage*, 265.
[19] See *The Constitutions of the Society of Jesus and Their Complementary Norms*, Constitutions, n. 288 (p. 124).

goodness of God, and since all creation is "being saved" and brought back to God through the dying and rising of Jesus, creation is intimately involved in the healing and redemption of humans. Would not Ignatius include it in the mission of humans to win the world for Christ? Nature, to be sure, has not sinned but it is affected by human sin and it can reveal to us the results of sin. Care for nature is implicated in care for humans, and is part of the mission of the risen Lord to restore all things in God.[20]

On further reflection, however, a new model for the God–world relationship seems to be needed to reinforce the belief that not just human beings but all of material creation will somehow experience resurrection, unending life with the triune God. Aquinas and other medieval

---

[20] In a 1998 talk on ecology given in Zimbabwe ("Our Responsibility for God's Creation") Fr. General Kolvenbach noted this connection: "Ignatius understands clearly that if God and the human person are not in a proper relationship this will have serious consequences in the biosphere. He invites the retreatant to 'an exclamation of wonder and surging emotion, uttered as I reflect on all creatures—the heavens, the sun, the moon, the stars, and the elements, the fruits, the birds, fishes and animals—on how they have allowed me to live and have preserved me in life.' (*SpEx*, n. 60) In the time of Francis and even of Ignatius, humanity was not in possession of the powerful means which today threaten the environment. From Ignatius' 'cry of wonder' we move today to a 'cry of horror.' In the words of John Paul II, 'Instead of fulfilling his role of collaborator with God in the work of creation, man acts independently of God and ends up by provoking the revolt of nature, more dominated than governed by him' (Centesimus Annus, n. 37)."

theologians found multiple reasons to affirm the presence of God in creation,[21] but they were reluctant likewise to say that material reality exists in God, shares the divine life. Admittedly, if not just the souls of human beings but likewise their bodies participate in the resurrection, then the rest of physical reality should likewise be capable of participation in the divine life. But how is this to be understood without implicitly endorsing pantheism, the functional identity of God and the world?

In the early nineteenth century the notion of panentheism came into vogue as a model for the God–world relationship. Since God is infinite and the world is finite, then somehow the world must exist in God even as it remains ontologically independent of God. But it always remained unclear how this could be the case without either the world being absorbed into God or God being identified with the world. One promising new possibility is based upon the premise that interrelated subjects of experience co-create a common field of activity even as they necessarily remain distinct from one another as independent subjects of experience. Thus they experience a dynamic unity in diversity in and through their shared field of activity. One can apply this model of intersubjectivity to the doctrine of the Trinity and propose that the three divine

---

[21] See, for example, Thomas Aquinas, *Summa Theologica* I, 8, 3.

persons co-generate an all-encompassing field of activity both for their internal relations to one another and for the world of creation, given their free choice to include creatures within the divine life. Furthermore, if all the persons and things of this world are aggregates or "societies" of dynamically interrelated subjects of experience as the British/American philosopher Alfred North Whitehead has urged,[22] then one can further claim that these same creatures by their ongoing interrelation constitute varying fields of activity proper to their own level of existence and activity and, most importantly, can be included within the field of activity proper to the divine persons or the "divine matrix."[23] In this way, every creature unconsciously participates in the trinitarian life of God from the first moment of its existence. Likewise, it shares in the transformation of the created order effected by Jesus' resurrection. Hence, whenever or however that creature ceases to exist in the present world of space and time, it can nevertheless continue to exist within the di-

---

[22] See, for example, Alfred North Whitehead, *Process and Reality: An Essay in Cosmology*, corrected ed., edited by David Ray Griffin and Donald W. Sherburne (New York: Free Press, 1978) 18, 34–35.

[23] See Joseph A. Bracken, SJ, *The Divine Matrix: Creativity as Link between East and West* (Maryknoll, N.Y.: Orbis, 1995) 52–69, 128–40. Likewise by the same author, *Christianity and Process Thought: Spirituality for a Changing World* (West Conschocken, Pa.: Templeton Foundation Press, 2006). Both books represent adaptations of Whitehead's philosophy to classical Christian beliefs.

vine communitarian life, albeit in a transformed state through somehow saying Yes to the free gift of the divine persons.

Key to this model of the God-world relationship is that matter and spirit are not opposed to one another but rather dialectically interrelated. Matter is the self-expression of spirit, even of the divine spirit insofar as the three divine persons express themselves in and through sharing a structured field of activity both with one another and with all their creatures. Created subjects of experience, in turn, co-constitute finite fields of activity for their ongoing interrelation and are simultaneously incorporated from moment to moment into the all-encompassing divine field of activity. Creation is thus a vast network of subfields of activity within the divine field of activity which Scripture names "the Kingdom of God." All this is possible because unlike substances in classical metaphysics, fields can be layered within one another and even interpenetrate without losing their ontological integrity as separate fields of activity. Likewise, the interrelated subjects of experience which in each case make up a given field of activity never lose their ontological independence of one another even as they together co-constitute from moment to moment that same field of activity. The three divine persons, in other words, can thus include all their creatures within the Kingdom of God as an ongoing, ever-changing divine-creaturely reality. Keeping this scheme in mind, we can now find new meaning and significance in the final meditation of the *Spiritual Exercises*.

Contemplation to Attain God's Love

Of all the *Spiritual Exercises* the *Contemplatio* would seem most clearly related to the environment. God is certainly present in all creation, "in the plants giving them life, in the animals giving them sensation, etc." (*SpEx*, n. 235). Yet, better to understand its meaning, we need to grasp its function in the Exercises. Ignatius himself gave no indication of how the *Contemplatio* was related to the Exercises. Like the Principle and Foundation, the *Contemplatio* has often been treated abstractly as a purely philosophical reflection—to become better aware of nature, the sun, the woods, etc. as God's creation. Seen that way, it could be placed anywhere in the Exercises, and in fact it was variously understood. It could be first, it could be last or it could be employed at each moment in the Exercises. Yet carefully looking at its content—that the *Contemplatio* is a prayer rather than simply a mental reflection—we see that it presupposes the unitive way, a mystical death to self and grounding in God. This would make it the culmination of the *Spiritual Exercises*, which is the position of Cusson[24] and the position we also are taking. Ignatius, after all, saw the Risen Lord Jesus in creation, not just the embodiment

---

[24] See Cusson, *Biblical Theology and the Spiritual Exercises*, 312–16.

of a philosophical principle. He experienced this vision by the Cardoner and we saw how it remained with him at the time of his Diary and letters. The *Contemplatio* presupposes a theology of the Risen Lord, which in turn presupposes the self-emptying and self-giving love of the Trinity in the work of creation and redemption. Ignatius' two prenotes to the *Contemplatio* should be seen in this light.

That "the lover communicates with the beloved what he or she has" (*SpEx*, n. 231) is not just a philosophical reflection on love. It is grounded in faith as we see from Scripture. The Father, for example, gives everything to the Son: "All power in heaven and earth has been given to me" (Matthew 28:18); "*all is given* to the Son that he might give all to the Father, that God may be all in all" (1 Corinthians 15:27-28). And further, this glory given to Jesus He gives to his disciples (John 17:22-23). God's infinite love is a total self-giving love revealed in the resurrection of Jesus. That is why Ignatius can say with assurance "the lover communicates with the beloved what he or she has." And further, it is a love shown in deeds, not just words. Jesus fulfills the "work" given by the Father and reveals His Glory (John 17). And we are to love as he loved, to "perform" all that Jesus commands (Matthew 28:20) and thus build on rock, not sand (Matthew 7:24-27). We are to "bear fruit" (John 15:8) by laying down our lives for others (John 15:12-13). What is needed is not just faith, but faith "working itself out in love"

(Galatians 5:6). This active love springs from the resurrection "sending" of the disciples. Thus the *Contemplatio* extends the grace of resurrection to humans and to the whole of creation.

In fact, as Michael Buckley has argued,[25] the *Contemplatio* can be seen as a synthesis of each Week of the Exercises. Contemplation is not static but a participation in the action of God in history and in our own lives. The purpose of the *Contemplatio* is developmental. We are to gain "interior knowledge" (*SpEx*, n. 233) of the good that we have received so that we in turn can serve God "in all things." We learn love by being loved. Each point of the *Contemplatio* begins with God and moves to our self-gift in response. We learn by doing, not just contemplating.

In the First Week, for example, we come to understand that we are created for God and that all is given to us so as to help us to serve God. Sin, however, is ingratitude. So healing from sin results in a growing sense of gratitude for creation and redemption which moves us in the Kingdom meditation to want to serve in return. Thus The First Point of the *Contemplatio* (*SpEx*, n. 234) urges us to be grateful for God's gifts of creation and redemption and concludes with "Take, Lord, and receive . . . ." All is gift. In the Second Week God enters history in Jesus' Incarnation and walks with us. We too are invited to walk with

---

[25] See Michael Buckley, "The Contemplation to Attain Love," *The Way Supplement* 24 (1975) 92–104.

Jesus and reform our lives accordingly. So The Second Point of the *Contemplatio* calls us to see how God dwells in all creatures. Creation and redemption mediate God's very being. Again, we conclude with "Take, Lord, and receive . . . ." All is "holy." In his Passion in the Third Week, Jesus "labors" for our redemption and we too are urged to labor with him. Hence, in The Third Point of the *Contemplatio* Ignatius calls us to see how God "labors" in all things, working out creation and salvation. We respond by offering ourselves ("Take, Lord, and receive . . ."). All is "sacred history." Finally, in His resurrected life in the Fourth Week Jesus transcends history and is one with the Father. From there he consoles us and intercedes for us. So in the Fourth Point of the *Contemplatio* we are to see how all things (like Jesus) come from God and return to God. We rest in the depths of God, and again respond with our whole selves. We love God for who God is. All "reveals" God.

Moreover, given this understanding of the basic structure of the *Contemplatio*, we can see how the Four Points in the *Contemplatio* represent a progressive purification of the "three powers of the soul" (memory, understanding and will) so as to be rooted and grounded in God's love as revealed in Jesus. The exercise of the "three powers," after all, pervades the whole Exercises.[26] It is

---

[26] See Lambert Classen, "'The Exercise with the Three Powers of the Soul,'" 237–71, for a fine presentation of this theme.

mentioned in the First Week (*SpEx*, n. 50ff), but it is also behind the contemplations of the Second Week and following; for the retreatant is to "see the people" (memory), "hear what they say" (understanding) and "see what they do" (will) in light of God's truth. Finally, in the *Contemplatio* each point concludes with the *Suscipe,* where we offer our memory, understanding and will to God as a total gift of ourselves, and receive, so to speak, God's memory, understanding and will—God's total self-gift of love—in return. This purifies our whole inner life and makes us a channel of God's love in all things. From this perspective, each point can be looked at as a purification of a different power of the soul, and the final point as a universal vision of all things proceeding from God and returning to God.

Thus, in the First Point, our memory is purified and healed by gratitude. Memory means how we make ourselves present to reality. By memory we transcend time, as St. Augustine notes in chapter 10 of his Confessions. Our "memory" can be wounded. We can remember only the hurts and rejections of the past, or deny memory of traumatic experiences. Through therapy or prayer for healing, memories can resurface in the context of love. Then even wounds and rejections can lead to gratitude as uniting us to Jesus. Gratitude is a sign that a memory is fully healed.[27] When we re-

---

[27] See Matthew Linn and Dennis Linn, *Healing of Memories* (New York: Paulist, 1974) esp. chapter 7: "Replacing Hurt with Love by Becoming Thankful for a Painful Memory."

member everything in the light of God's love, we are filled with gratitude. Applied to the environment, we become aware that "the Land is mine" (Leviticus 25:23). It belongs to God and is a gift to humans who are "meek," that is, fully surrendered to God. As we give our memories to God, God returns them with a new awareness of love. Then, with gratitude, we can realize how we are served by all creation. "For those who love God, everything works for good" (Romans 8:28).

Likewise, the healing of understanding can be linked with the Second Point, namely, God "dwelling" in all things. What is the meaning of what happens to us or what is given to us? Why do we experience rejection or failure or are put in a family that is abusive and dysfunctional, or in an environment that is devastated by misuse? Why does God allow creation to be so exploited and devastated by humans? We are filled with questions that seem to have no answers, as Job was filled with questions. Yet the only "answer" Job received was a new experience of God—God's "presence" takes us beyond sin and self-centeredness to the heart of creation. The only "answer" we Christians receive is the mystery of the cross of Christ. We meet Jesus in precisely those traumatic experiences. God is forming Jesus in us, who "dwells" in each experience of joy or pain and in our brokenness or that of the environment, and becomes present to us in it. We experience God's vulnerable love at the heart of each creature and in every event as we get in touch with our own vulnerability. Like St. Francis protecting the worm as revealing Jesus, we see creation through the eyes of God's love as revealed in the gift of Jesus unto death. This heals our understanding. We get to the bottom of things (stand under things) and find their true meaning.

Further, there is a correlation of the Third Point of the *Contemplatio* with the purification of the third power of the soul, the will. According to Ignatius, God "works" and "labors" in all things, by giving and conserving them in being, but also by entering into the depths of our sin and woundedness. Jesus "works" as God "works" (John 5:17) and his "work" is to glorify God by a life that reveals God as self-giving love (John 17:4). God shepherds his sheep (Ezekiel 34), gives birth as a mother (Isaiah 49:15), fights for His people (Exodus 15:3; Isaiah 42:13), creates as a potter (Jeremiah 18:1-6), gives the promised Land. God consoles, teaches, guides "into all truth" (John 14:25-26). Each image is on-going, an ever-present "caring" that is the "work" of the Holy Spirit abiding with us, forming Christ in us, uniting us with one another and with all creation in the one Body of Christ till all be submitted to him and he to the Father (1 Corinthians 15:27-28). When our will is purified, it will be "tuned in" to this working and laboring of God in creation. Like Jesus, we also will "labor" (Third Week) and "console" (Fourth Week), bringing all of creation to image forth God's love.

The Environment in the Spiritual Exercises

Finally, we are to see every gift as coming from God and returning to God, as Ignatius saw at the Cardoner and ever after. Ignatius invites the retreatant to see the whole universe as springing from God, existing in God and through Jesus (and ourselves working under his banner) being returned to God. "All power" has been given to Jesus. Human stewardship of creation has been restored in Him. What is needed now is for his followers to live by that truth, to say "Yes" to Jesus' on-going leadership. In that sense, the *Contemplatio* is a bridge from the Exercises to everyday life. As we see everything as coming from God, existing in God and returning to God, we choose to be part of that movement by praying the *Suscipe*. Whatever role Jesus' Lordship plays in the transformation of creation, we are called to be part of it. We are called to receive creation (nature and all things) as gift from God and through our co-working to liberate it to be all that God intends it to be.

Conclusion
Our Call to Serve God in All Creation

IN assuming a human nature, Christ united to himself both humanity and the material creation, and through his cross and resurrection he regrounded creation in Trinitarian life. In the vision of Teilhard, Christ is the physical center of the Universe and God wants this grace to spread out and deeply unify humans and the physical universe. In terms of the neo-Whiteheadian scheme sketched above, creation comes forth from God, unconsciously exists in God even now, and eventually returns to God so as to live the divine life forever in a transformed condition. Creation is thus the gradual unification and complexification of what was sheer multiplicity or pure potentiality at the moment of the "big bang" act of creation.

The world as a result is a graded hierarchy of fields within fields. Each new field of activity unifies all that went before in a new synthesis, at the same time as it respects and even further perfects the lower-level field of activity in its own right. Thus the integrated field of activity corresponding to the animal kingdom integrates the various

Conclusion

fields of activity proper to vegetative life and even further differentiates the latter, even as plant life integrates and further differentiates the world of inorganic compounds. Likewise, the field proper to human activity (for Teilhard de Chardin, the *noosphere*) reflects on all that went before it and reaches out to inquire into the dynamism of the whole universe. Each level thus embodies both a particular type of integration together with a potency for higher integration because of its continuing multiplicity. At the human level of existence and activity, of course, multiplicity can likewise lead to disorder and even chaos in the world of creation because of human sin. But these centrifugal tendencies have in principle already been overcome by the Incarnation, Death, and Resurrection of the Son of God/Son of humanity—Jesus Christ. Since the human field of activity includes in its scope the whole underlying universe, Jesus Christ is the ultimate integration of the whole cosmos. Yet each higher union also further differentiates what went before, as Teilhard de Chardin repeatedly affirmed in his phrase "union differentiates." So Christ should likewise be seen as the ultimate point of differentiation and individuation within creation; each creature is itself in a new way in Christ. Finally, Christ as God incarnate integrates all of creation into the ongoing communitarian life of the three divine persons. The end result is a cosmic community of interrelated subjects of experience, beginning with the divine persons but extending to all their creatures, within the "space" or common field of activity created by their dynamic interaction.

Ignatius' mystical experience as seen in the Spiritual Exercises and in his Diary accords well with this vision of the progressive unification of all things in Christ and through Christ in the triune God. "All things are created for humans," he writes, "to help them attain the service of God" (Principle and Foundation). Other creatures "serve" us in spite of our sinfulness (First Week). Yet they are all created by God, exist in God during their time on this earth and reveal God's beauty. They are not simply means to human ends, but precious in their own right. For us to serve God's glory is to care for all creatures as God does. God indwells and continues to work in all creatures and we are to bring our actions into harmony with God's (*Contemplatio*).

We know today better than ever before that material creation is affected by human self-centeredness, blindness and sin. This very exploitation is now recoiling back on humans. We can see the desert we are creating, the defilement of God's beauty and fruitfulness in creation. Yet Scripture says that creation remains God's even though the earth's current disordered state reveals our sin and calls loudly for our conversion back to God's love. When we see God's love as self-emptying love in service of releasing all creation into the praise of God (as St. Francis and St. Ignatius clearly did), then we see that our spiritual "ascent" to God's love is not so as to transcend this world, but to gain the freedom to "return" and serve the whole—that all creation might reveal God's self-emptying love. There is, in other words, a movement of ascent in the Spiritual Exercises, but only so as to attain the necessary freedom of spirit and detachment that we might become loving servants of one another. Thus, the "labor" we are to undertake in service of our King is "to go against our self-love" in order that God's all-pervasive redemptive love may direct and empower our lives.

This implies a passionate commitment to protect and care for all creation as the temple of God's presence. We are called to restore the beauty of creation—human and material. As Isaiah says: "No more shall people call you 'Forsaken,' or your land 'Desolate,' but you shall be called 'My Delight,' and your land 'Espoused.' for the Lord delights in you, and makes your land his spouse" (Isaiah 62:4). "In place of the thornbush, the cypress shall grow, instead of nettles, the myrtle. This shall be to the Lord's renown, an everlasting imperishable sign" (Isaiah 55:13). The renewal of the earth is a sign of the Lord's glory, and we are to be servants of that glory.

Bibliography

Berry, Thomas. *The Dream of the Earth*. San Francisco: Sierra Club Books, 1990.

Bowman, Leonard J. "The Cosmic Exemplarism of Bonaventura." *Journal of Religion* 55 (1975) 181–98.

Bracken, Joseph A., SJ. *Christianity and Process Thought: Spirituality for a Changing World*. West Conschocken, Pa.: Templeton Foundation Press, 2006.

———. *The Divine Matrix: Creativity as Link between East and West*. Maryknoll, N.Y.: Orbis, 1995.

———. *Jesuit Spirituality from a Process Perspective*. Studies in the Spirituality of Jesuits 22/2. St. Louis: Seminar on Jesuit Spirituality, 1990.

———. *Society and Spirit: A Trinitarian Cosmology*. Selinsgrove, Pa.: Susquehanna University Press, 1991.

Brueggemann, Walter. *The Land: Place as Gift, Promise, and Challenge in Biblical Faith*. 2d ed. Overtures to Biblical Theology. Minneapolis: Fortress, 2002. (1st ed. Philadelphia: Fortress, 1977.)

Buckley, Michael. "The Contemplation to Attain Love." *The Way Supplement* 24 (1975) 92–104.

Christiansen, Drew. "Notes on Moral Theology." *Theological Studies* 51 (1990) 64–81.

Clarke, Thomas E. *The Eschatological Transformation of the Material World According to St. Augustine*. Woodstock, Md.: Woodstock College Press, 1956.

Classen, Lambert. "'The 'Exercise with the Three Powers of the Soul' in the Exercises as a Whole." In *Ignatius of Loyola: His Personality and Spiritual Heritage, 1556–1956: Studies on the 400th Anniversary of His Death*, edited by Friedrich Wulf, 237–71. Modern Scholarly Studies about the Jesuits, in English Translations 2. Saint Louis: Institute of Jesuit Sources, 1977.

Cusson, Gilles. *Biblical Theology and the Spiritual Exercises.* St. Louis: Institute of Jesuit Studies, 1994.

Dalmases, Candido de. *Ignatius of Loyola, Founder of the Jesuits: His Life and Work.* Translated by Jerome Aixal. St. Louis: Institute of Jesuit Sources, 1985.

Fox, Matthew. *Breakthrough: Meister Eckhart's Creation Spirituality.* Garden City, N.Y.: Doubleday, 1980.

———. *The Coming of the Cosmic Christ: The Healing of Mother Earth and the Birth of a Global Renaissance.* San Francisco: Harper & Row, 1988.

———. *Creation Spirituality: Liberating Gifts for the Peoples of the Earth.* San Francisco: HarperSanFrancisco, 1991.

Fritsch, Al, SJ, and Robert Sears, SJ. *Earth Healing: A Resurrection-centered Approach.* Livingston, Ky.: ASPI, 1993. [Appalachia: Science in the Public Interest, P.O. Box 423, Rt. 5, Livingston, Ky. 40445.]

Galli, Mario von, SJ. *Living Our Future: Francis of Assisi and the Church Tomorrow.* Chicago: Franciscan Herald, 1972.

Ganss, George, SJ, editor. *Ignatius of Loyola: Spiritual Exercises and Selected Works.* New York: Paulist, 1991.

Gilson, Etienne. *The Christian Philosophy of St. Thomas Aquinas.* Translated by L. K. Shook. New York: Random House, 1956.

Guibert, Joseph de. *The Jesuits—Their Spiritual Doctrine and Practice: A Historical Study.* Translated by William J. Young. Chicago: Institute of Jesuit Sources, 1964.

Haas, Adolf. "The Mysticism of St. Ignatius according to His Spiritual Diary." In *Ignatius of Loyola: His Personality and Spiritual Heritage, 1556–1956,* edited by Friedrich Wulf, 164–99. Modern Scholarly Studies about the Jesuits, in English Translations 2. St. Louis: The Institute of Jesuit Sources, 1977.

Habel, Norman C. *The Land Is Mine: Six Biblical Land Ideologies.* Overtures to Biblical Theology. Minneapolis: Fortress, 1995.

Habig, Marion A., editor. *St. Francis of Assisi: Writings and Early Biographies.* Chicago: Franciscan Herald, 1973.

Bibliography

Hessel, Dieter, and Larry Rasmussen, editors. *Earth Habitat: Eco-Justice and the Church's Response.* Minneapolis: Fortress, 2001.

Ignatius of Loyola. *The Constitutions of the Society of Jesus.* Edited and translated by George E. Ganss, SJ. St. Louis: Institute of Jesuit Sources, 1970.

———. *The Spiritual Exercises of St. Ignatius.* Translated with a commentary by George E. Ganss, SJ. Chicago: Loyola University Press, 1992.

———. *The Spiritual Journal of St. Ignatius of Loyola.* Translated by William J. Young. Rome: CIS, 1979.

Lampe, G. W. H. "The New Testament Doctrine of *ktisis*." *Scottish Journal of Theology* 17 (1964) 449–62.

Landes, George. "Creation and Liberation." *Union Seminary Quarterly Review* 33 (1978) 79–89.

Linn, Matthew, and Dennis Linn. *Healing of Memories.* New York: Paulist, 1974.

Mitchell, Donald W. *Spirituality and Emptiness: The Dynamics of Spiritual Life in Buddhism and Christianity.* New York: Paulist, 1991.

Murphy, Nancey, and George F. R. Ellis. *On the Moral Nature of the Universe: Theology, Cosmology, and Ethics.* Theology and the Sciences. Minneapolis: Fortress, 1996.

Niebuhr, Reinhold. *Moral Man and Immoral Society: A Study in Ethics and Politics.* New York: Scribner, 1932.

Nigg, Walter. *Warriors of God.* New York: Knopf, 1959.

Santmire, H. Paul. *Nature Reborn: The Ecological and Cosmic Promise of Christian Theology.* Minneapolis: Fortress, 2000.

———. *The Travail of Nature: The Ambiguous Ecological Promise of Christian Theology.* Philadelphia: Fortress, 1985.

Schillebeeckx, Edward. *Jesus: An Experiment in Christology.* Translated by Hubert Hoskins (New York: Crossroads, 1981.

Sears, Robert T., SJ. "Resurrection Spirituality and Healing the Earth." *Review for Religious* 49 (1990) 163–77.

Teilhard de Chardin, Pierre. *The Future of Man.* Translated by Norman Denny. New York: Harper & Row, 1959.

———. *The Phenomenon of Man.* Translated by Bernard Wall. New York: Harper & Row, 1965.

Toolan, David, SJ. "'Nature Is a Heraclitean Fire': Reflections on Cosmology in an Ecological Age." *Studies in the Spirituality of the Jesuits* 23/5 (November 1991).

White, Lynn. "Historical Roots of Our Ecological Crisis." *Science* 155 (1967) 1203–7.

Whitehead, Alfred North. *Process and Reality: An Essay in Cosmology.* Corrected edition. Edited by David Ray Griffin and Donald W. Sherburne. New York: Free Press, 1978.

Wolter, Hans. "Elements of Crusade Spirituality in St. Ignatius." In *Ignatius of Loyola: His Personality and Spiritual Heritage, 1556–1956: Studies on the 400th Anniversary of His Death,* edited by Friedrich Wulf, 97–134. Modern Scholarly Studies about the Jesuits, in English Translations 2. Saint Louis: Institute of Jesuit Sources, 1977.

Wulf, Friedrich, editor. *Ignatius of Loyola: His Personality and Spiritual Heritage, 1556–1956: Studies on the 400th Anniversary of His Death.* Modern Scholarly Studies about the Jesuits, in English Translations 2. Saint Louis: Institute of Jesuit Sources, 1977.